Get Along, Get It Done, Get Ahead

Get Along, Get It Done, Get Ahead

Interpersonal Communication in the Diverse Workplace

Geraldine E. Hynes
Sam Houston State University

BEP BUSINESS EXPERT PRESS

Get Along, Get It Done, Get Ahead: Interpersonal Communication in the Diverse Workplace
Copyright © Business Expert Press, LLC, 2015.

First published in 2015 by
Business Expert Press, LLC
222 East 46th Street, New York, NY 10017
www.businessexpertpress.com

ISBN-13: 978-1-63157-130-5 (paperback)
ISBN-13: 978-1-63157-131-2 (e-book)

Business Expert Press Corporate Communication Collection

Collection ISSN: 2156-8162 (print)
Collection ISSN: 2156-8170 (electronic)

Cover and interior design by S4Carlisle Publishing Services Private Ltd., Chennai, India

First edition: 2015

10 9 8 7 6 5 4 3 2 1

Printed in the United States of America.

Dedication

To Jim, who has been my center for more than 45 years

Abstract

This book goes beyond descriptions of culture-bound business practices or prescriptions for valuing diversity. Because intercultural dynamics take place in domestic as well as multinational companies, all business professionals must be competent in interpersonal communication. This practical approach presents techniques for managers to reduce diversity miscues, strategies to respond to uncomfortable conversations, and innovative ways to bridge cultural gaps. Managers will learn how to build rapport and promote constructive behaviors in a diverse work environment. The book also offers guidelines for communicating internally as well as with external stakeholders, including a section on how to develop employees' communication competencies through formal training.

Keywords

managerial communication, diversity, teams, supervisory communication, interpersonal communication, business communication, cultural competence, training

Contents

Preface

I grew up on the west side of Chicago in a tough neighborhood. How tough? I remember one morning on the way to school when I spotted a dead body in a parking lot—the victim of a gangland-style shooting—surrounded by police officers. I kept walking. Mom and Dad had warned me not to talk to strangers.

Now I live on a cattle ranch in Texas and teach at a university in a nearby small town. How I got here is another story, and maybe even another book. As you can imagine, life here is very different from Chicago. For one thing, people are friendlier. A woman in my fitness class once told our group that she'd lived all her life in Texas except for the three months when her husband's employer had transferred the family to California. "I hated it there," she complained. "No one ever talked to me while we waited in line at the checkout. I made Cody take us back home to Texas." "Where I grew up," I commented, "we called that minding your own business."

I'm getting used to acquaintances as well as strangers telling me to have a nice day, except on Thursday, when they tell me to have a great weekend. I do know something about diverse greeting customs. After all, I've traveled widely and even lived abroad, so I've experienced a range of cultures. Once I had a Japanese student who stood whenever I entered the classroom. That made me feel good. Another time I had a French student who shook hands with me after every class. So I'm no longer startled when my Texan students hug me, though it still makes me uncomfortable.

The point I'm making here is that cultural diversity is a fact of life, and a lot depends on how we respond to it. We all encounter people who are different from us, and since we usually think our ways are the right ways, then their ways must be wrong. Whether it's a family member, a neighbor, or a club member, developing a relationship will be challenging because of cultural differences. Of course, you might decide you don't like them because of what they eat (or don't eat) or what they wear (or don't wear) or because of what they believe (or don't believe), and no relationship develops at all. But what about when you're at work? You might think, "Well, I have to work with them, but I don't have to like them or socialize with them." If you're a manager of a diverse workgroup, you might think, "I'll just treat them all alike and ignore their differences." But neither avoidance nor denial will lead to what is known as cultural competence.

The purpose of this book is to demonstrate that, first of all, diversity in the workplace is a competitive advantage, not a roadblock. Secondly, this book offers a number of practical communication strategies that will help you capitalize on the benefits of workplace diversity. Effective intercultural communication impacts both the financial and the operational performance of a business. A well-trained workforce can operate successfully in a multicultural environment. However, many companies are not doing enough to overcome cultural and communication barriers. This book suggests communication behaviors that will maximize cultural competence.

The old paradigm of "managing cultural differences" has evolved beyond simple prescriptions, do's and taboos, that apply primarily when working in foreign countries. Today the goal is to develop skills and strategies that can be applied to daily interactions in any work environment. The ideas in this book will foster interpersonal relationships, which lead to increased job satisfaction, loyalty, and commitment, all of which lead to improved productivity and organizational success. By learning how to get along, you will learn how to get it done, and ultimately to get ahead.

Geraldine E. Hynes

PART 1

Communication Cornerstones

CHAPTER 1

Diversity Appreciation

If you're at work right now, take a look at the people around you. There's Ben, who's still a PC person, despite your repeated attempts to show him the superiority of a Mac. There's Isabelle, who irritates you because she's so closed-minded and stubborn about politics. Over there is Joey, who refuses to admit that *Star Wars* is the all-time greatest blockbuster movie series.

You don't have a whole lot in common with any of the people you work with, never have and probably never will. The workplace is a loose affiliation of folks with widely different religions, political preferences, worldviews, backgrounds, and interests. Each of us is closed off from the others behind a wall of belief that we're right and they're just wrong. Maybe you've formed a little tribe of likeminded people with whom you can relax over lunch and review Sunday's game. If so, you probably think that work would be lots easier if only these people were on your team instead of the goobers.

This chapter argues that workplace pluralism is not only a fact of life, it's a competitive advantage. Further, the chapter outlines strategies that you, as a manager, can adopt to capitalize on the advantages and minimize the disadvantages of workforce diversity. The trick is not to work *against* employees' differences, but to work *with* them for business success. Finally, the chapter suggests ways you can improve your communication competence when interacting with two particularly tricky populations on the job: age-diverse and gender-diverse workers.

Benefits of Workplace Diversity

If you're a tough, skeptical manager in this values-obsessed age, you've probably asked yourself, "Why can't I simply run my department in a fair, ethical way, focus on performance, treat everyone the same, and let the rest take care of itself? Why should I do anything special to 'embrace diversity'?" There are some good answers to your questions. Performance is probably the most important one. Diverse companies tend to be superior performers because they realize that the best way to meet their business imperatives is to have all people as part of the talent pool—here in the United States and around the world.

But there are several other important reasons that managers should leverage diversity. Let's examine four that are undeniable:

Benefits of diversity:

1. Stronger customer connections
2. Innovative solutions
3. Superior performance
4. Values-driven policies

Stronger Connections with a Diverse Customer Base

Executives at top companies consider it obvious that being a good employer of minorities and under-served populations will be good for marketing and customer relations in all sorts of ways. A company that has a reputation for valuing all people does have an advantage. If about 34 percent of U.S. consumers—the total for Asians, Blacks, Latinos, and Hispanics nationwide—suspect they won't be welcome at your company, you're headed for trouble.

Grasping the idea that many potential minority customers are highly aware of a company's minority-friendliness—and make buying decisions partly on that basis—is critical. One company that recognizes the importance of meeting the needs of ever-evolving markets is Massachusetts Mutual Life Insurance (MassMutual), a 163-year-old financial services company. Their efforts to weave diversity and inclusion into company culture are not just a business strategy; they're a defining goal.

"Here at MassMutual, we know that the demographics of our nation are changing," said Sylena Echevarria, assistant vice president of U.S. Insurance Group, Client Services and head of the Association for Latinos at

MassMutual. "As you have a more diverse consumer and customer base, your business activities, the initiatives you kick off, the products that you offer, the type of service you deliver, the interactions you have with your customers—those all need to change and evolve as well."

"If we don't reflect the demographics of our policy owners, we may not make the best decisions for them," Echevarria explained. "We may not understand what it is that they're looking for in order to do business with us or to retain their business."[i]

Morgan Stanley is a global financial services company with more than 55,000 employees operating in 43 countries. Like MassMutual, Morgan Stanley has formalized the effort to reach diverse markets. For example, the company supports a Multicultural Client Strategy Committee, which is tasked with focusing on the needs of clients from different backgrounds and perspectives. A key realization is the idea that many potential minority customers are highly aware of a company's minority-friendliness—and make buying decisions partly on that basis.

Simply put, when the employees on the front lines look like the customers and think like the customers, it's easier to develop trusting relationships that lead to doing more business.

More Innovative Solutions

Francis Bacon, a 15th century philosopher and father of the scientific method, said, "Those who will not apply new remedies must expect new evils, for time is the greatest innovator." Companies preparing to compete in tomorrow's global economy must rely on diverse thinkers who can create innovative solutions to new problems. Diversity is a competitive advantage because different people approach similar problems in different ways. Thus, diverse groups make better decisions.

As discussed in the previous section, Morgan Stanley is a company that fosters diversity in its workforce because it strengthens relationships with its customer base. In addition, Morgan Stanley believes that diverse workgroups are better at creative problem solving. Jeff Brodsky, Chief Human Resources officer, said, "We believe a diverse workforce brings innovative thinking and enables us to serve our clients in a way that delivers the best financial solutions."[ii]

Improved Performance Effectiveness

A third benefit of workforce diversity is improved performance. Government agencies came to that realization early. One example of a federal government agency that fosters diversity to enhance performance effectiveness is the National Aeronautics and Space Administration (NASA). The team that developed Rover, the device that crawled around the surface of Mars as part of the Mars Pathfinder Mission in 2000, exhibited true diversity. The 20-person team included three women, one African-American male, and an East Indian male, according to Donna Shirley, Head of the Mars Pathfinder Mission. Speaking at an Innovative Thinking Conference in Scottsdale, Arizona, Shirley described the team as being diverse on other dimensions as well, including thinking style, experience, creativity, and personality. She pointed out that the diversity of talents enabled the Pathfinder project to fulfill its mission with a budget of $264 million, "roughly the budget for the film, 'Waterworld.' And it got better reviews."

Diversity is good for the bottom line.

Multinational corporations now agree with nonprofits and governmental agencies that diversity is linked to performance. What began for many companies as an effort to meet governmental and legal requirements has evolved into a strategic priority for success. Businesses with a committed, long-term, systematic, and strategic approach to diversity consistently show better performance.[iii]

Ford Motor Company is an example of a corporation that has created metrics to prove the impact of diversity initiatives on the company's overall business strategy. At Ford, for instance, employee resource groups (ERGs) demonstrate their value to the bottom line by tracking the number of vehicles members sell through the company's Friends and Neighbors vehicle discount plan. Michele Jayne, Personnel Research Manager for Ford, said, "Achieving a diverse workforce and effectively managing this workforce can yield huge benefits."[iv]

Simply put, diversity is good for the bottom line.

The Right Thing to Do

Superior performance may be the most practical reason to welcome diversity, but occasionally the moral argument is heard—making a company especially friendly to minorities is worth doing simply because it's the right and ethical thing to do. Organizations have a duty to act as corporate citizens, regardless of the economic implications.

Tony Burns, former CEO of Ryder Trucks and onetime president of the Urban League, believed that his company's efforts toward minorities were good business, but he also said that he launched initiatives to diversify his employee base without knowing for sure that it would pay off. So why did he launch them? "Because it was the right thing to do."[v]

Today's organizations are held to a standard of consistency between their stated values and their actual policies. When a company's mission and vision statement includes a clause about diversity, then they are expected to walk the talk. Empty gestures toward inclusiveness are quickly exposed, and reputations suffer.

To summarize, it's a safe bet to predict that companies will continue to foster diversity among their workforce and business partners, for at least four reasons: stronger customer connections, innovative solutions to business problems, superior performance, and the moral imperative. The next section of this chapter focuses on concrete actions that companies are taking to foster diversity. Hopefully, you will find some good ideas to take back to work.

Strategies for Welcoming and Supporting Diversity

There are no secrets to successful recruiting, supporting, and leveraging diversity in business environments. Companies with enviable track records have implemented a range of strategies that you and your organization might also be able to adopt. The days are long gone when inclusiveness meant merely serving fajitas in the company cafeteria on Cinco de Mayo (a national holiday in Mexico commemorating their victory over French forces at the Battle of Puebla on May 5, 1862). The following paragraphs describe five strategies for welcoming diversity and explain how they apply in certain companies.

Ways to support diversity:

1. Recruit diverse employees
2. Promote diversity at leadership levels
3. Establish employee support groups
4. Establish mentorship programs
5. Partner with diverse companies

Recruit Diverse Employees

Massachusetts Mutual Life Insurance Company and Morgan Stanley are companies that strive to reach out to community partners and to recruit and retain workforces that incorporate a range of cultures, backgrounds, experiences, and perspectives. Both businesses actively recruit talent from historically under-represented backgrounds and communities. Recruiters search for potential employees as early as high school. They partner with prestigious universities, campus diversity groups, and other organizations committed to diversity, such as the National Association of Black Accountants.

Ensure Diversity at the Top Levels

The leadership of truly diverse organizations will also reflect diversity. MassMutual's efforts to diversify the workforce extend to the very top. Women and people of color compose nearly half of all seats on the board of directors. The company's Diversity Recruitment Strategy engages Asian, Hispanic, Latino, African-American, women, those with disabilities, and members of the LGBT communication as decision makers in crafting initiatives to recruit, retain, develop, and cultivate future leaders.

Prudential, another financial services multinational company, is led by a diverse board of directors. According to Gale Britton, vice president of diversity and inclusion, the directors include two non-U.S. citizens, one African-American, one Asian-American, and one Hispanic. Three of the 12 directors are women. Furthermore, women compose nearly 40 percent of Prudential's leaders.

The National Football League represents another kind of business that uses an aggressive approach to ensuring diversity at the leadership level. Their Rooney Rule requires teams to interview at least one minority candidate for every head coach or general manager opening.[vi]

Establish Employee Networking Groups

To provide channels that will carry a diversity of ideas and thought upward, MassMutual established a Women's Leadership Network and eight employee resource groups (ERGs), support groups for specific employee populations. ERGs organize opportunities to celebrate and share their heritage with others in the company. Under-represented groups sometimes believe that the best way to advance is to work hard and blend in, but ERGs take a different approach, allowing them to leverage their backgrounds, speak their minds, and share ideas. MassMutual's Sylena Echevarria summarizes the value of her Latino ERG thusly: "For someone who used to shy away from sharing my heritage, I am now able to represent my community and have a seat at the table."

Another example of a company-supported employee networking group is Morgan Stanley's work-life integration program. This group addresses working parent and family concerns as well as the need for increased flexibility. Other employee networking groups provide opportunities for workers to celebrate their cultures and support local organizations while increasing positive exposure and relationship building.

Prudential is a third company that creates and supports employee networks whose charge is to promote social activities and professional development. Among the groups is "VetNet," for active members of the military, veterans, and veterans' partners. Another is the "Employee Association of Gay Men, Lesbians, Bisexuals, Transgenders, and Allies (EAGLES), a group that helped conduct research on the financial and legal concerns of same-sex couples and LGBT parents.

Establish Mentor Programs

As support groups for employees of similar backgrounds, MassMutual's ERGs provide mentors and leadership programs. Echevarria says, "I never thought I'd be in the position I am today because there weren't people around me when I was growing up who worked in a professional setting that I could look to share experiences."

"Morgan Stanley is very much an apprenticeship culture," said Jeff Brodsky, Chief HR officer. Among their mentoring programs is "Return to Work," a 12-week paid internship, pairing participants with senior-level leaders based on their skills, experiences, and interests.

Comprehensive apprenticeships are available that include skills development, stretch assignments, mentoring, and coaching for women and minorities. The company also sponsors high-profile leadership summits that offer employees opportunities to learn from top talent such as their 2014 Women's Leadership Summit for 300 female financial advisers and managers.

Seek Diversity Among Business Partners

The diversity benefits certainly operate in business-to-business and even business-to-government partnerships. One example of a company that actively seeks out vendors and business partners from broad backgrounds and varying perspectives is Prudential. Their stated goal is to do business with vendors that reflect the demographics of local markets. Prudential actively seeks bids and proposals from business enterprises that are owned by minorities, women, veterans, service-disabled veterans, representatives of the LGBT community, and people with disabilities.

Communicating with Diverse Workers

Once you've recognized that workplace diversity contributes important advantages to an organization and you've identified ways that you can welcome and support a pluralistic work environment, you may be wondering how all of these affect your daily communication patterns. After all, the purpose of this book is to help you improve your managerial communication skills.

Diversity sensitivity leads to effective managerial communication.

If your communication behavior reflects your sensitivity to differences, it will be more successful and effective. This section describes how two very common types of workplace diversity—age and gender—influence managers' interaction styles and how you can improve your ability to communicate with each population.

Age Diversity

Americans are living longer, and the average employee is getting older. For the first time ever, four generations are working together. These groups include the shrinking sector of Silents who are in their 70s but still working, the large post-World War II Boomer generation, Gen-Xers born in the late 60s to about 1980, and the Millennials born after 1980. Every generation is different, and generation gaps are natural. If you are a Gen-Xer or a Millennial, you may well find yourself managing people old enough to be your parents or even your grandparents. How awkward is that?

What do older workers fear? Let's step into their shoes for a minute and make a list:

- New technology
- Younger employees
- Discrimination
- Obsolescence
- Changes in the workplace

Baby Boomers (in their late 50s or 60s) have always felt dominant, perhaps because of their sheer numbers. They are notoriously poor savers, so many can't afford to retire. Besides, many are still vigorous, healthy, and intellectually curious. They seek stimulation and opportunities to continue contributing to society. In short, they aren't yet ready to step aside, and they expect their younger managers and coworkers to respect them for their age and experience.

Are there any value differences or attitudinal differences between older workers and younger managers? Yes, there appear to be several that are relevant to workplace relationships, as shown by the following comparison of Boomers and Millennials.

Generational differences in values:

- Attitudes toward authority
- Attitudes toward work
- Importance of seniority
- Attitudes toward organizations and groups

- *Attitudes toward authority*—Boomers came of age in the 1960s, when challenging authority was a rite of passage. They marched for social justice and sat in for peace. Although most people in their generation eventually became part of, or even leaders of, The Establishment, insurrection is still considered an option.
- *Attitudes toward work*—Boomers get up each morning, get ready, and go to work. To them, work is a place, not an activity. After work, they go home, where they don't like to do work. Millennials may not physically get to the workplace as much, but you can be sure that they checked their messages before brushing their teeth this morning.
- *Importance of seniority*—Boomers expect respect because they've come so far and cast such a long shadow all their lives. Surviving, whether it's the Vietnam War or 9/11, counts.
- *Attitudes toward organizations and groups*—Boomers are joiners. Membership in professional associations and workgroups is valued, and they wear their Rotary Club lapel pins with pride. They show up for high school reunions; younger generations don't have to go to reunions because they stay in touch with classmates on social media. They believe in teamwork.

If you manage older employees who exhibit "retired on the job" (ROTJ) behaviors, here are some communication tips:

- Get at the roots of the problem rather than working from assumptions

- Be specific about inappropriate behaviors; don't generalize or stereotype
- Allow the employees to vent and express themselves
- Demonstrate empathy

Managing older subordinates with performance problems may require that you seek more creative solutions. Think of ways to capitalize on their life experience by offering mentoring opportunities and special assignments. To help keep their skills up to date, provide more job sharing, job rotation, and training. Working in teams with younger peers will allow each generation to recognize the other's strengths and worldviews.

Strategies for managing older workers:

- Mentoring opportunities
- Special assignments
- Job sharing
- Short-term projects
- Job rotation
- Training
- Heterogeneous teams

Now let's briefly look at the reverse situation—older managers in charge of a younger generation of workers. Generational tensions seem especially strong between managers in their 40s (Generation X) and subordinates in their 20s (Millennials). According to Harvard Business School researchers, Gen-Xers started working when the economy was slow, and their career paths were rocky. Feeling vulnerable, they made personal and family sacrifices to achieve success. Today, these young employees are less willing to sacrifice their time with their families. They expect to be evaluated for productivity, not hours at their desk, especially when tech tools make their geographic location irrelevant. Their loyalties lie with their social network rather than their job, and they do not fear change.

Strategies for managing younger workers:

- Flextime
- Focus on goals, not methods
- Technology tools
- Variety
- Long-term projects
- Heterogeneous teams

By 2020, fully half of the U.S. workforce will be of the Millennials' age. Their values and attitudes are already influencing the workplace in interesting ways. For instance, new corporate office buildings are designed for maximum natural light, with high ceilings, outdoor areas, and common spaces rather than small offices and cubicles. The emphasis is on "we" space rather than "me" space.[vii] Companies such as ExxonMobil and Anadarko currently provide amenities such as fitness centers, jogging trails, bicycle racks, and wellness centers to attract and keep younger employees.

Clearly, when values clash between bosses and subordinates, effective communication across the generational divide becomes even more important. As a manager, you must be sensitive to age diversity because of its implications for employee retention, harmony, and workplace efficiency.

Gender Diversity

Over the past 30 years, researchers have closely examined how men and women communicate differently at work, but results have been inconsistent because of the complexity of contributing factors. Social scientist Deborah Tannen not only found strong evidence for gender differences but made a case for supporting the differences in communication styles of men and women. In doing so, she also presented interesting reasons men and women have difficulty communicating with each other. These reasons include both innate traits and learned behavior.[viii] Some of the gender differences in workplace conversations that Tannen identified are shown in Table 1.1, along with example statements.

Table 1.1 Men and Women in Conversation

Men	Example	Women	Example
Ask for information	Who's the expert on this software?	Ask for help	I need help learning this software.
Use report-talk	These are the facts.	Use rapport-talk	Most of us are happy with this solution.
Use powerful language	That won't work.	Use powerless language	I may be wrong, and stop me if you disagree, but I think there may be roadblocks.
Complain	Your missing the deadline wrecked my project's schedule.	Apologize	I'm sorry to hear that you can't meet the deadline.

As the Table shows, differences often exist between men and women as to how they handle various communication situations:

- *Asking for Information and Help*—Men are more likely to ask for information, while women are more likely to ask for help.
- *Report-talk versus Rapport-talk*—Men are more likely to stick to the facts and information, while women are more likely to talk about relationships.
- *Powerful versus Powerless Language*—Men often use fewer words, which makes them seem powerful and confident, while women often add disclaimers, modifiers, and requests for agreement, which make them seem tentative.
- *Apologies versus Complaints*—Men are more likely to complain when they are dissatisfied, while women are more likely to seek explanations, excuses, and even assume responsibility for the situation.

In addition to these differences in speaking styles, researchers have identified differences in listening styles. Women are more likely to listen to affirm both the relationship and the person who is speaking, zooming in on an emotional level and being empathic. In contrast, men tend to listen for the facts and information in a message and are less comfortable handling its emotional content. They are more likely to listen for solutions and are more willing to give advice than empathy.[ix]

Such differences in communication style between genders don't appear to be diminishing, and they are important because of the increasing gender diversity of the workforce. Both men and women will have difficulty succeeding if they cannot successfully communicate with each other.

The U.S. Bureau of Labor Statistics projects that women will be the majority of the workforce by 2022.[x] Women are also moving into management in greater numbers. According to the U.S. Census Bureau, women filled 51.5 percent of management, professional, and related occupations in 2012.[xi] Furthermore, the number of women serving as corporate officers in the top ten Fortune 500 companies doubled in less than 20 years and was at 17 percent in 2014.[xii] According to Sheryl Sandberg, COO of Facebook and author of the bestseller, *Lean In*, when more women lead, performance improves. Companies with more gender diversity have more revenue, customers, market share, and profits.[xiii]

If you've noticed that men and women communicate differently at work, you've also probably experienced the breakdowns that can result. Effective managers must be sensitive to gender differences and make special efforts to adjust their communication. Furthermore, female managers are typically more risk-averse than men, take a longer-term perspective, and are more relationship-oriented. You're better off considering such gender differences to be complementary rather than problematic, since research shows that diversity in work teams leads to better outcomes.

Summary

The first cornerstone of communication competence in today's diverse workplace is recognition of its benefits. Major benefits of a diverse workforce include stronger customer connections, more innovative solutions, superior performance, and values-driven policies. Top organizations apply a number of strategies for welcoming and supporting diversity such as recruiting diverse employees, promoting diversity at leadership levels, establishing employee support groups, establishing mentorship programs, and partnering with diverse companies.

Two types of diversity are particularly important for today's managers: age and gender. Relevant values and mindsets that differ across generations include attitudes toward authority, attitudes toward work, the importance of seniority, and attitudes toward organizations. Major differences in communication style between genders don't appear to be diminishing, and they are important because of the increasing gender diversity of the workforce. Both men and women will have difficulty succeeding if they cannot successfully communicate with each other.

Endnotes

i. J. Feld (2014, November 9). "Leadership in Diversity and Inclusion," *New York Times Magazine,* pp. 54–8.

ii. J. Feld (2014, November 9). "Leadership in Diversity and Inclusion," *New York Times Magazine,* p. 56.

iii. T. Kochan, K. Bezrukova, R. Ely, S. Jackson, A. Joshi, K. Jehn, et al. (2003). "The Effects of Diversity on Business Performance: Report of the Diversity Research Network," *Human Resource Management* 42, pp. 3–21.

iv. M.E.A. Jayne, R. Dipboye (2004, Winter). "Leveraging Diversity to Improve Business Performance: Research Findings and Recommendations for Organizations," *Human Resource Management* 43, no. 4, pp. 409–24.

v. G. Colvin (1999, July 19). "Outperforming the S&P 500: Companies that Pursue Diversity Outperform the S&P 500. Coincidence?" *Fortune* 140, no. 2. Available at http://money.cnn.com/magazines/fortune/fortune_archive/1999/07/19/263098/index.htm.

vi. "Silicon Valley's Diversity Problem" (2014, October 5). *New York Times,* p. SR10.

vii. N. Sarnoff (2014, June 13). "Younger Workers Crave 'Sense of Place' on the Job," *Houston Chronicle,* p. D1.

viii. D. Tannen (2007). *You Just Don't Understand: Women and Men in Conversation* (New York, NY: William Morrow).

ix. J.T. Wood (2013). *Gendered Lives: Communication, Gender, and Culture,* 10th ed. (Boston: Wadsworth), p. 127.

x. M.Toossi (2013, December). "Labor Force Projections to 2022," *Monthly Labor Review,* Retrieved from www.bls.gov/EMP

xi. "Labor Force, Employment, and Earnings" (2012) (U.S. Census Bureau), Statistical Abstract of the United States, Table 616, p. 393.

xii. S. Krawcheck (2014, March 24). "Diversify Corporate America," *Time*, pp. 36–7.

xiii. A.Grant (2013). *Give and Take: A Revolutionary Approach to Success* (New York, NY: Viking Press), pp. 58–9.

CHAPTER 2

Cultural Competence

Part One lays two "cornerstones" or basic concepts that are the foundation on which the framework of this book is built. The first cornerstone is *diversity appreciation*. In Chapter 1 we discussed the increasing diversity of the workforce and considered four competitive advantages that diversity offers. We also examined communication strategies that you, as a manager, can adopt to capitalize on the advantages of workforce diversity.

This chapter describes our second cornerstone, *cultural competence* (Figure 2.1). Diversity brings with it different cultural norms, leadership styles, and communication patterns, so you can see the critical link between cultural competence and your success as a manager. If you know how to navigate among cultural differences, you will be equipped to develop positive relationships with your employees, leading to productivity, profits, and organizational success.

Figure 2.1 Cornerstones of the Sequence for Success

What Is Cultural Competence?

Corporate response to the increasing diversity of the workforce varies widely, but cultural competence is generally valued. Cultural competence is defined as being "comfortable working with colleagues and customers from diverse cultural backgrounds."[i] Cultural competence is known as the "third wave" of diversity thinking—after affirmative action and inclusion. Indeed, today's employers consider intercultural skills as a top consideration when hiring. In a recent survey of 318 executives from both private sector and nonprofit organizations, 96 percent agreed that it's mandatory for their new hires to be culturally competent.

Reactions to diversity in business:

1. Affirmative action
2. Inclusion
3. Cultural competence

Briefly, a culturally competent manager understands that culture profoundly affects workplace behavior and attitudes. Furthermore, a culturally competent manager knows how to navigate relevant cultural differences in order to maximize workers' loyalty, satisfaction, productivity, and ultimately the bottom line. The Economist Intelligence Unit recently surveyed 572 executives in multinational organizations around the globe. The business leaders overwhelmingly agreed that cultural competence improves revenues (89 percent), profits (89 percent), and market share (85 percent). The executives widely agreed that managerial communication skills are essential for workforce productivity.[ii]

Why Culture Matters

Let's take a closer look at the notion of culture so we can see why it's such an important factor in managerial success. Culture is what we grow up in. Beginning in childhood, we learn acceptable behaviors, customs, and habits. We also adopt the beliefs, values, and moral attitudes of the society in which we mature. A body of common understanding develops. We know what to expect, and we know what is expected of us.[iii]

Culture is what we grow up in.

Defined in such a way, culture includes the religious system to which we are exposed, the educational system, the economic system, the political system, the legal system, morals, recreational outlets, mores governing dress and grooming, standards of etiquette, food and how it is prepared and served, gift-giving customs, quality and quantity of communication among the people, greeting practices, rituals, modes of travel available, as well as the many other aspects of our lives.

There is some evidence that culture can even affect our personalities. For instance, a series of studies of people who spoke both Spanish and English showed that switching languages significantly affected personality variables such as extraversion (or assertiveness), agreeableness (superficial friendliness), and conscientiousness (achievement).[iv] Bilingualism is becoming more common in the United States, especially among the younger generation. According to the U.S. Census Bureau, Millennials are the most diverse generation in history, with one in four speaking a non-English language at home.

Furthermore, culture can influence the way we see the world. If you show pictures of a monkey, a panda, and a banana to someone from Japan and ask which two go together, chances are that the Japanese will pick the monkey and the banana, because the former eats the latter. Show the same pictures to someone from Great Britain and she or he will select the panda and the monkey, because they are both mammals. Westerners typically see classifications where Asians see relationships.

There is strong evidence that these differences in worldviews begin in childhood. In another study, Japanese and American children were asked to look at a tank of large fish, small fish, and some aquarium plants and rocks. When they were asked what they saw, the Japanese kids described the groups of fish and the environmental elements. The Americans talked about the big fish.[v] The researchers concluded that the collectivist Japanese culture encourages youngsters to focus on groups, while the individualist U.S. kids learn early on to focus on standouts (Figure 2.2).

Figure 2.2 What do you see in this picture?

Malcolm Gladwell explored the importance of culture in his best-seller, *Outliers: The Story of Success.* He concluded, "cultural legacies are powerful forces. They have deep roots and long lives. They persist, generation after generation, virtually intact … and we cannot make sense of our world without them."[vi]

A Closer Look at Cultural Differences

What are the "deep roots" of cultural differences that Gladwell was referring to? One of the most extensive studies of cultural differences was conducted at IBM Corporation by a Dutch management thinker, Geert Hofstede. He surveyed more than 116,000 IBM employees in 40 countries. A massive statistical analysis of his findings revealed six dimensions of national culture as shown in Figure 2.3: power distance, uncertainty avoidance, individualism/collectivism, masculinity/femininity, high and low context, and monochronic/polychronic time.[vii] Examining Hofstede's framework can help you anticipate and then solve possible problems caused by misunderstandings between employees from different cultures.

Power distance indicates the extent to which a society accepts the fact that power is distributed unequally. It is reflected in the values of both the more powerful and less powerful members of the society. The Philippines, Venezuela, and Mexico are countries with high power distances; and Denmark, New Zealand, the United States, and Israel are a few of the countries with low power distances.

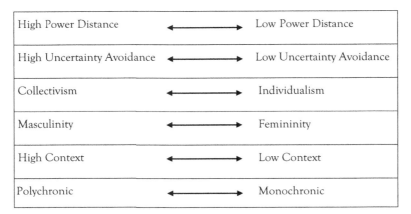

Figure 2.3 Hofstede's Dimensions of Cultural Differences

High/low power distance: The extent to which society accepts the unequal distribution of power.

A manager in a culture with high power distance is seen as having dramatically more power than a subordinate would have. This manager, who usually is addressed respectfully by title and surname, might favor a controlling strategy and behave like an autocrat. For instance, within the British Houses of Parliament, lawmakers can move to the head of the line at restaurants, restrooms, and elevators, while clerks, aides, and secretaries who work in Parliament must stand and wait. In a culture with a lower power distance, however, a manager is seen as having little more power than a subordinate, is often addressed by first name, takes her place in line, and manages by using an equalitarian communication strategy.

Uncertainty avoidance relates to the degree to which a society feels threatened by uncertainty and by ambiguous situations. People within such a society try to avoid these uncertainties and ambiguous situations by providing greater career stability, establishing and following formal rules, not allowing odd ideas and behaviors, and believing in absolute truths and the attainment of expertise. Greece, Germany, England, and Japan have strong uncertainty avoidance, while Hong Kong, Denmark, the United States, and Sweden have weak uncertainty avoidance.

High/low uncertainty avoidance: The extent to which society feels threatened by ambiguity.

If you are managing subordinates whose culture values uncertainty avoidance, you will have difficulty getting them to embrace change. Most likely, they will prefer the status quo. To reduce resistance, try to get your people involved in the new strategy and highlight the benefits of change.

On the *individualism/collectivism* dimension, *individualism* suggests a loosely knit social framework in which people are expected to take care of themselves and their immediate families only. *Collectivism*, on the other hand, is a tight social framework in which people distinguish between in-groups and out-groups. They expect their in-group (relatives, clan, organization) to take care of them; and because of that, they believe they owe absolute loyalty to their in-group. The United States, Australia, and Great Britain are the most highly individualistic countries on Hofstede's scale, while Pakistan, Colombia, Nigeria, and Venezuela are more collectivist countries.

> Individualism/collectivism: The extent to which society prefers loyalty to the group over loyalty to the individual.

If you are a manager from an individualistic culture and you are participating in negotiations with business professionals from a collectivist culture, you will be frustrated when they resist making decisions. They must first collaborate to reach consensus. You may ask to talk to a "decision maker," but there won't be one. Try to be patient while the other group spends so much time in conference.

Masculinity/femininity is the fourth Hofstede dimension. Masculinity includes assertiveness, the acquisition of money and things, and not caring about the quality of life. These values are labeled masculine because, within nearly all societies, men scored higher in these values than women. Japan, Austria, and Mexico were among the most masculine societies. Feminine cultures, by contrast, value family, children, and quality of life. Denmark, Sweden, and Norway are considered feminine cultures.

> Masculinity/femininity: The extent to which society values quality of life.

Consider the following example. In the United States, people are judged at least partly on their ability to make a good salary. Frequently, this judgment precludes traditional U.S. feminine values of caring for children. Despite the passage of the Family Leave Act in 1993, the majority of U.S. working men and women do not take the full time they are eligible for when dealing with family and medical problems.

The fifth cultural difference in Hofstede's model is *context*. In a *high-context* culture, much information is gathered from the physical context or environment or the person's behavior. People look for meaning in what is not said—in the nonverbal communication or body language; in the silences, the facial expressions, and the gestures. Japan and Saudi Arabia are high-context countries, as are Chinese- and Spanish-speaking countries.

High/low context: The extent to which society gathers information from the environment.

In a *low-context* culture, the most information comes from the language. In such a culture, communicators emphasize sending and receiving accurate messages directly, usually by being highly articulate. Canada and the United States are low-context cultures. As you might suspect, negotiations between low-context and high-context cultures can be tricky. The value of contracts and documents used in business-to-business transactions will vary by culture. In high-context countries, agreements are sealed with handshakes between those with strong personal relationships.

The sixth dimension of cultural differences, according to Hofstede, is *monochronic versus polychronic time*. In a monochronic culture, such as Germany, the United States, and most westernized nations, we talk about saving time, wasting time, making time, and spending time. We measure time by the clock, often in nanoseconds. In hyper-punctual countries such as Japan, pedestrians walk fast and bank clocks are accurate. In Western businesses we read quarterly returns and define "long-term" projections as those going out 3 to 5 years into the future. Time is linear.

Monochronic/polychronic: The way a society perceives time.

In polychronic cultures, such as Spain, Latin America, and most Asian countries, time just *is*. These cultures trace their roots back thousands of years. Time is measured by events, not the clock. Thus, promptness diminishes in value, and being "late" is a sign of status. In Ecuador, for instance, politicians, military officers, and business people are less punctual than blue-collar workers are.

People in polychronic cultures are more patient, less interested in time management or measurement, and more willing to wait for their rewards than those in monochronic cultures. And the fact that polychronic cultures typically are less economically successful than monochronic cultures is not a compelling reason for change.

Developing Cultural Competence

All of us can benefit from increasing our understanding of cultural differences. Now that we have explored the deep roots of some of these differences, as described in Hofstede's model, you can see that culture has a profound effect on each of us. As a culturally competent manager, you will recognize that culture determines why your employees

- Prefer authoritarian or democratic leadership
- Need more or less personal space and privacy
- Perceive punctuality as important or not
- Are future-oriented or look to the past
- Are factual or intuitive in decision making
- Value individual achievement or loyalty to the group
- Focus only on the words or on everything except the words

When observing employee conflicts, other managers may not notice that the underlying issue could be cultural. They might think, "What's wrong with you? You shouldn't be so upset." But culturally competent managers will recognize that cultural background strongly influences the way employees respond to any situation.

Once you recognize how pervasive a person's culture is and how different it may be from yours, you can then begin to appreciate the complexity of good management. If you want to succeed in our highly competitive global marketplace, you will need to see and accept things as others see and accept them.

Cultural differences can affect work relationships in domestic as well as multinational corporations. Subcultures in the United States, primarily labeled by geographic region, may affect workers' behavior, communication style, and values just as much as national cultures do. My personal story as a Yankee who works in Texas provides an example of domestic cultural differences, as I described in the Preface of this book.

Understanding your workforce includes recognizing and respecting the cultural roots of their attributes, whether international or domestic, and trying to adapt to their culturally based values and behaviors. As a culturally competent manager, you will take better advantage of this type of diversity and see it as an asset to be valued, not a liability to be dealt with.

Barriers to Cultural Competence

The biggest roadblock to cultural competence is our own cultural values. From an early age, we are taught that our way of doing things is the right way, and everyone who is different is wrong. This bias against difference is natural and normal, not pathological, and mostly subconscious. But every day our biases determine what we see and how we judge those around us. We have biases about almost every dimension of human identity.

Bias is a normal psychological reaction to difference.

We are attracted to and tend to like people who are similar to us, not different from us. The perceived similarities may or may not be real. When people think they're similar, they expect to have positive future interactions. Therefore, the discovery of similarities and differences is crucial in developing relationships. Here's how it works:

Think about a time you had to interview a job candidate. When the candidate walked in and greeted you, you immediately noticed her gender, race, dress, appearance, speech patterns, handshake, and even body size. And you immediately formed judgments based on those outward factors. If you perceived those factors to be similar to yours, you probably formed a positive impression of the candidate. If you perceived those factors to be different from yours, you probably formed a negative impression. As the interview went along and you gained more information about her background, experiences, and skills, you probably paid most attention to the information that confirmed your first impressions and disregarded the information that conflicted with them. That normal mental process can lead to bias and discrimination. It can also lead to costly hiring mistakes.

Overcoming the Barriers

How can you avoid scenarios like the one above? Howard Ross, the founder of Cook Ross, an international diversity consulting company and author of *Everyday Bias* and *Reinventing Diversity*, suggests four strategies for developing cultural competence:

1. *Recognize and accept that you have biases.* Bias is a normal psychological phenomenon. Rather than feel guilty about your biases, take responsibility for them. Once you accept them, you can begin to limit their impact.
2. *Practice "constructive uncertainty."* Slow down decision making, especially when it affects other people.
3. *Try to interact regularly with and learn about people you feel biased against.* Exposing yourself to positive role models will reduce the risk of discrimination.
4. *Look at how you make decisions.* Consider the impact of environmental factors, time of day, and your physical and emotional state in order to identify barriers to perception.[viii]

Strategies for developing cultural competence:

1. Recognize and accept that you have biases.
2. Practice constructive uncertainty.
3. Learn about people that you feel biased against.
4. Look at how you make decisions.

Let's apply Ross's four strategies to the job interview scenario described earlier. If your first impression of the candidate is negative because you perceived her outward characteristics (age, appearance, race, gender, voice, handshake) to be different from yours, what should you do? The first step is to recognize your bias and the possibility of premature judgment. Next, deliberately decide that you won't jump to conclusions. Ask questions and listen closely to her responses. Try to penetrate well below the surface so you can exchange information more accurately. Bring in another interviewer whose opinions you respect and then compare impressions afterward.

It's true that similarities make it easier to build relationships at work. It's also true that most work groups develop their own subculture over time; members adapt their values, behaviors, attitudes, and even appearance so they fit into the workgroup and gain a sense of belonging. However, different traits and outlooks will give your team balance, opportunities for growth, and possibilities for learning new ways of thinking. Becoming aware of your mental processes will help you to become culturally competent so you can make better decisions, whether it's about hiring or anything else. You will read more about these processes in Chapter 4.

Three Cases of Corporate Cultural Competence

After examining the roots of cultural differences and what's involved in becoming culturally competent, let's look more closely at how three very high-profile corporations respond to their multicultural environments.

Our first case is Walmart, the largest retailer in the United States, Canada, and Mexico, and the second largest in Britain. Worldwide, more than seven billion people shop at a Walmart each year. But Walmart stores failed in Germany. Why? For one thing, many Germans found the idea of a smiling greeter at the entrance to be off-putting. In fact, many male shoppers interpreted it as flirting. For another thing, German labor unions objected to Walmart's non-union hiring practices.

Walmart also has been insensitive to cultural values in Brazil and Mexico, where the company's stores focused sales campaigns on items the people in those countries don't use—golf clubs and ice skates. Cultural competence was in short supply in Korea, too, where Walmart built stores with shelves so tall that customers had to use ladders to reach the products.[ix] These examples of failed management and sales tactics at Walmart demonstrate what can go wrong when decision makers lack cultural competence.

Our second case is Honda Motor Company, one of the most successful multinational companies in the world, employing 140,000 people globally. Astonishingly, Honda has been profitable every year since its inception in 1949. The Honda business model, known as lean manufacturing, is built on Eastern principles that emphasize

- Simplicity over complexity
- Minimalism over waste

- A flat organization over a complex hierarchy
- Perpetual change

Staying true to this cultural framework is the secret of the company's excellent performance. Just how does Honda do it? Jeffrey Rothfeder spent 5 years researching the company and describes in his book, *Driving Honda*, how the organization's processes align with their bedrock principles. Take one of these principles, for example—"respect individualism." Given the Japanese culture's emphasis on teamwork, this principle is surprising. Most companies encourage workers to team up toward a common goal. But Honda views collaboration from the vantage point of the individual, not the team. Honda sees the individual's capabilities, decision making, knowledge, and creativity as the source of the group's performance. In short, Honda practices cultural competence.

This quote from the founder, Soichiro Honda, captures the profound respect for individualism:

"In the ocean you see a bunch of fish and they're going every which way. And something happens, a stimulus happens where one lines up, then another, and another, until they all line up and they go together in the same direction, perfectly. Later, they separate again to find their own way and nourishment. That's also how successful teams and businesses work."[x]

This emphasis on individualism and creativity translates into physical aspects of the workplace. Honda factories are flat environments. The offices are open bullpens with desks; there are no private dining rooms—just a cafeteria, and no reserved parking spaces. Employees have no job descriptions. The result, according to Rothfeder, is enthusiastic, efficient, productive workplaces with high morale and frequent communication.

Our third case study of cultural competence is Zappos, the largest online retailer of shoes, clothing, and accessories. Amazon bought the company for $1.2 billion in 2011. Similar to the Honda work environment, Zappos's corporate headquarters in Las Vegas has no offices, although there's a nap room. CEO Tony Hsieh eliminated job titles, instead creating a flat organizational chart.

Zappos requires its managers to spend significant time listening to employees. In his best-seller, *Delivering Happiness*, Hsieh wrote that he required his managers to spend 20 percent of their time away from their desks. The upshot is more opportunities for people to enjoy their work and to be self-reliant and responsible. Hsieh estimates that because of Zappos's flat and lenient culture, workers are 20 to 100 percent more productive.[xi]

Hsieh recognizes that a workforce with different likes and dislikes, personalities, and ways of interpreting the world is the best source of improvements. As in Honda's culture, with its emphasis on respect for the individual, Zappos capitalizes on employees' cultural differences. The principle of individualism is tied to salaries and all other business activities. It's not just window dressing.

These three cases, Walmart, Honda, and Zappos, demonstrate what can go right when a company aligns and recalibrates its strategic goals with the company's basic principles, and what can go wrong when it doesn't. The takeaway is that maintaining a consistent corporate culture and being sensitive to the cultural environment are fundamental aspects of doing business.

Culture and Communication Style

At this point you may be thinking, "All this sounds true enough; it goes along with what I've seen in my own career. But the concept of cultural competence is pretty abstract. My job description doesn't cover establishing and maintaining the company's culture. What are some concrete actions I can take to enhance my cultural competence and help the company to succeed?"

The answer is that cultural competence is reflected in your communication style. Every day, when you interact with coworkers, subordinates, customers, suppliers, and other stakeholders, everyone's culture acts as a lens through which your messages are filtered. Similarly, their messages to you are filtered through your own cultural lens. Being sensitive to unintended distortions of the messages' meanings equals cultural competency.

Cultural competence is reflected in communication style.

Cultural Sources of Misunderstanding

Various cultures view feedback differently. For example, managers in the United States and Europe typically prefer direct communication; they deliver feedback that is explicit, honest, and authentic. In Asian cultures, communication is expected to be more vague and indirect, and managerial feedback is more likely to be nuanced because bluntness might injure the employees' self-esteem. Furthermore, Asian cultures value silence. Silence, like talk, communicates.[xii]

Cultural sources of misunderstanding in conversations:

- Degree of directness
- Silence
- Loudness and pitch
- Appropriate topics
- Touch
- Eye contact

Here is an example of communication style differences that are culturally based. It is part of a conversation between a Chinese police officer in Hong Kong and his supervisor:

Chinese police officer: My mother is not well, sir.
English supervisor: So?
Chinese police officer: She has to go into hospital.
English supervisor: Well?
Chinese police officer: On Thursday, sir.

The meaning of this exchange is clouded by cultural differences in communication style. The Chinese officer is hoping that his boss will realize what he wants and offer this before he has to ask for it. In British English, however, it is more typical to start with the request and then give reasons if required. So, the English version of this conversation would be something like this:

Chinese police officer: Could I take a day off please?
English supervisor: Why?

Chinese police officer: My mother is not well and must go to the hospital.[xiii]

Typical British English speech patterns are similar to U.S. patterns in their degree of directness. When people from Asian cultures are more indirect, Westerners may view them as evasive. A Westerner lacking cultural competence might impatiently prod the speaker to "get to the point." On the other hand, a culturally competent Westerner would understand that the Asian roundabout pattern is used to avoid the risk of hurt feelings and is therefore often a more relationship-sensitive communication style.

Naoki Kameda, a prominent Japanese business communication researcher, explains that the indirect communication style represents important values, based on the "3Hs":

- Humanity—warm consideration for others
- Harmony—efforts not to hurt the feelings of others
- Humility—modesty[xiv]

By comparison, a direct style seems pretty self-centered, doesn't it?

Communication Style and Empathy

It's easier to communicate with others when you understand and agree with the cultural values behind their communication style preferences. Furthermore, if you can empathize with the other person, share his feelings, and relate to his intentions, then you might even adopt his communication style during the interaction. All you have to do is ask yourself, "If I were on the receiving end, how would I react to this message?" Then adjust your communication style so the receiver's understanding is closer to what you intended. As you will read in Chapter 5, effective business communication leads to stronger relationships and feelings of empathy and trust. These emotional conditions, in turn, lead to improved performance, productivity, and organizational success.

> "Successful business communication is about 10 percent business and 90 percent human relations."
>
> —A. Wilson, 1975

Summary

Along with diversity appreciation, cultural competence is a cornerstone for getting along, getting it done, and getting ahead at work. Culturally competent managers understand that culture profoundly affects workplace behavior and attitudes, and they know how to navigate relevant cultural differences in order to maximize workers' loyalty, satisfaction, productivity, and the bottom line.

While bias against difference is natural and normal, it can restrict thinking and prevent the development of workplace relationships, empathy, and trust. Culturally competent managers recognize that culture is a lens that filters messages. They develop flexible communication styles to overcome barriers and increase shared meaning.

Endnotes

i. Hart Research Associates (2013). *It Takes More than a Major: Employer Priorities for College Learning and Student Success* (Washington, DC: Association of American Colleges and Universities).

ii. D. Bolchover (2012). "Competing Across Borders: How Cultural and Communication Barriers Affect Business" (The Economist Intelligence Unit Ltd. Report), p. 11.

iii. N. Sigband, A. Bell (1986). *Communicating for Management and Business*, 4th ed. (Glenview, IL: Scott Foresman), pp. 69–70.

iv. N. Ramirez-Esparza, S.D. Gosling, V. Benet-Martinez, J.P. Potter, J.W. Pennebaker (2006). "Do Bilinguals have Two Personalities? A Special Case of Cultural Frame Switching," *Journal of Research in Personality* 40, pp. 99–120.

v. R. Nisbett (2004). *The Geography of Thought: How Asians and Westerners Think Differently…and Why* (New York, NY: Free Press).

vi. M. Gladwell (2008). *Outliers: The Story of Success* (New York, NY: Little, Brown and Company), p. 175.

vii. G. Hofstede (1980). "Motivation, Leadership and Organization: Do American Theories Apply Abroad?" *Organizational Dynamics* Summer, pp. 42–63.

viii. H.J. Ross (2014, August 3). "An Appeal to Our Inner Judge," *New York Times*, p. D3.

ix. J.W. Neuliep (2012). *Intercultural Communication: A contextual Approach*, 5th ed. (Thousand Oaks, CA: Sage Publications), pp. 374–5.

x. J. Rothfelder (2014). *Driving Honda: Inside the World's Most Innovative Car Company* (New York: Portfolio/Penguin), p. 134.

xi. T. Hsieh (2013). *Delivering Happiness: A Path to Profits, Passion, and Purpose* (New York, NY: Grand Central Publishing).

xii. W.B. Gudykunst (1998). *Bridging Differences: Effective Intergroup Communication*, 3rd ed. (Thousand Oaks, CA: Sage Publications).

xiii. This example is from A. Kirkpatrick (2009). *World Englishes: Implications for International Communication and English Language Teaching* (Cambridge, England: Cambridge University Press) as reported in N. Kameda (2014). "Japanese Business Discourse of Oneness: A Personal Perspective," *International Journal of Business Communication* 51, no. 1, pp. 93–113.

xiv. N. Kameda (2014). "Japanese Business Discourse of Oneness: A Personal Perspective," *International Journal of Business Communication* 51, no. 1, p. 102.

CHAPTER 3

The Sequence for Success

So far, we've described two "cornerstones" or basic concepts that are the foundation for this book. The first cornerstone is *diversity appreciation*; Chapter 1 documented the increasing diversity of the workforce and explained why diversity is a competitive advantage for organizations.

The second cornerstone is *cultural competence*; Chapter 2 showed how differences in employees' cultural values, customs, and communication patterns require managers to be skillful in navigating among these differences. Culturally competent managers know how to develop positive relationships with diverse employees that will positively affect workers' loyalty, satisfaction, and productivity.

In Chapter 3 we build on these two cornerstones (Figure 3.1) to create a framework for the rest of the book. After reading this chapter, which completes Part One, you will see how managers who appreciate diversity and who have cultural competence are able to get along (Part Two), get it done (Part Three), and get ahead (Part Four).

Figure 3.1 Cornerstones of the Sequence for Success

Interpersonal Communication and Interpersonal Relationships

Getting along with peers, subordinates, bosses, customers, suppliers, and shareholders is mostly a matter of communication. To build strong relationships with all these constituencies you must interact with them regularly. As you will read in Chapter 4, there can be no relationship if there is no communication. Therefore, communication and work relationships are the first two building blocks for organizational success. We will set these building blocks on top of the two cornerstones already in place (Figure 3.2).

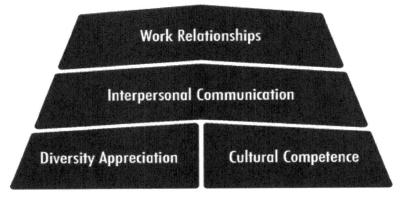

Figure 3.2 Building Blocks of the Sequence for Success

Let's think a little more about the impact of your interpersonal communication. If you're a manager, your daily interactions with your subordinates typically center on these 10 topics, right?

1. Procedures
2. Guidance
3. Policies
4. Work conditions
5. Work problems
6. Solutions to work problems
7. Deadlines, goals
8. Corrective feedback
9. Positive feedback
10. Raises, promotions, advancement

You might want to add to this list of topics, depending on your own unique situation at work, but these are the top 10 things that managers and subordinates talk about on the job. You already know that your communication style when interacting with your subordinates about these topics will significantly determine how well they do their job. Their performance depends on the clarity, accuracy, and timeliness of your instructions, information, and feedback.

But did you know that your communication style will also determine what they think about you as a boss? An interesting study of 363 adults with an average of 8 years of work experience focused on what they considered to be a "good boss." Contrary to what you might predict, the researchers found no evidence that the workers evaluated their bosses according to how the bosses used their authority, control, or power. Instead, the most important factor for judging their bosses to be good or bad was the extent to which the bosses showed appreciation, respect, or high regard for the workers. This factor is called "affiliation." By the way, sex did not seem to influence the workers' ratings of the quality of their supervisors. Both male and female workers rated both male and female superiors as "good" bosses if their communication was high on affiliation.[i]

Good bosses are affiliative.

Making an effort to develop relationships with your subordinates will make your job easier. Ever wonder why your people don't comply with your demands/requests? After all, you are the boss. Here's why: your job title may give you authority, also known as position power, but if you want to influence your direct reports, you also need personal power. Personal power derives from your credibility. The elements of managerial credibility are:

- Rank—position in the hierarchy
- Expertise—skill or knowledge
- Image—personal attractiveness
- Common ground—shared value
- Goodwill—personal relationships

It's that last item on the bulleted list that we're talking about here. Goodwill is how you get your people to put up with poor working conditions, long hours, stressful deadlines, and nasty customers. Goodwill is a product of personal relationships.

Position power = authority
Personal power = credibility

Relationships and Emotional Conditions

Let's add another building block to our Sequence for Success model, one that captures key emotional conditions caused by strong relationships. "Wait. Why should I worry about emotions and relationships with my employees?" you may ask. "I have to work with these people, but I don't have to like them." True. In fact, if you ever find subordinates and coworkers that you like well enough to become friends outside of work, that's a bonus. More often, however, the people we consider to be our friends will disappear from our lives when they (or we) leave the organization.

On the other hand, a strong case can be made for trying to develop positive relationships with your team and your subordinates, so that certain emotional conditions occur. Among these key emotions are loyalty, satisfaction, commitment, and trust. They are represented by the new building block in Figure 3.3. Notice that "liking" is not on this list of emotions. You can trust people without liking them. You can also feel loyal, satisfied, and committed to a job without liking the actual work.

Figure. 3.3 More Building Blocks of the Sequence for Success

Organizational commitment means that your people will:

- Identify with the organization's goals and values
- Want to belong to the organization
- Be willing to display effort on behalf of the organization[ii]

Research consistently shows that low organizational commitment leads to absenteeism, turnover, and unrest. On the other hand, high organizational commitment leads to trust, quality and quantity of communication, involvement, and productivity.[iii] Therefore, if you treat your employees well, they will work harder for you.

Emotional Commitment and Performance

Let's finish building the Sequence for Success model by adding another block that represents productivity and organizational success. The connection between job performance and key emotional conditions is well established. Figure 3.4 illustrates that when employees feel a sense of loyalty, commitment, job satisfaction, and trust, their productivity improves and, ultimately, the organization succeeds.

Want more evidence for the truth of this Success model—that communication and commitment ultimately lead to organizational success? In 2013, the Project Management Institute published results of their survey of 1,093 project managers, executives, and business owners who were involved in large capital projects worldwide. The business leaders agreed that *the most crucial success factor in project management is effective communication* to all stakeholders. Further, the study showed that highly effective communicators are *five times* more likely to be high performers than poor communicators, as measured by whether they finished the project on time, within budget, and according to the original goals.[iv]

If you're still not convinced that managerial communication leads to organizational success, here's even more evidence. In a 2012 review of 263 research studies across 192 companies, Gallup found that companies in the top quartile for "engaged" employees, compared with the bottom quartile, had 22 percent higher profitability, 10 percent higher customer ratings, 28 percent less theft, and 48 percent fewer safety incidents.[v]

Figure. 3.4 The Complete Sequence for Success Model

Employee Engagement

Employee engagement is a hot topic. Engaged workers are committed, involved, enthusiastic, and energized. Engaged workers typically are also high performers. Alarmingly, however, a 2013 Gallup survey showed that only 30 percent of U.S. employees describe themselves as engaged at work. Around the world, across 142 countries, the proportion of engaged employees drops to 13 percent. In short, most workers feel dissatisfied and discouraged. And their productivity suffers.[vi]

Engaged workers are committed, involved, enthusiastic, energized, and productive.

In the face of such overwhelming research findings, we must acknowledge that the way people feel at work profoundly influences how they perform. Managers who think that pay is the primary influence on performance haven't been paying attention. Although financial rewards are relevant—who among us would work for free?—the psychological and emotional rewards are what keep us on the job.

What drives engagement? In a word, communication. The Great Place To Work Institute found that employees enjoy working in an environment where they "trust the people they work for, have pride in what they do and enjoy the people they work with."[vii] Such positive work environments are typically characterized by open communication. While larger companies may expect their Communication Department to be responsible for broadcasting information internally and externally, most employees consider their managers to be the most important source of transparency. Managers are expected to share relevant information with subordinates; managers are responsible for promoting a sense of belonging and commitment, and helping their subordinates to understand the company's mission. These behaviors develop trust, which leads to employee engagement.[viii]

Facilitating Engagement through Communication

Step back for a minute so you can get the big picture and see where you are now. We started with acknowledging that today's workforce is incredibly diverse and that managers must be sensitive to the cultural differences people bring to the workplace. Upon those two cornerstones we built a model for success. The model illustrates that daily interpersonal communication leads to stronger relationships. Those relationships cause feelings of trust, loyalty, commitment, and job satisfaction. These important emotions motivate people to work harder and be more productive, which ultimately leads to the organization's success.

The most important implication of our Sequence for Success model is that managers must facilitate open, honest, and frequent communication.

"What?" you may ask. "If people are spending all their time talking, when are they going to get the job done?" While you may be tempted to tell workers to quiet down and get to work, discouraging workers from interacting with you or each other will backfire.

Companies that realize their workers are more productive if they have more social interaction are taking some simple steps to foster internal communication. Here are some examples. Bank of America observed that employees working in their call centers who had formed tightknit communications groups were more productive and less likely to quit. To increase social communication, the bank introduced a shared 15-minute coffee break each day. Afterward, call-handling productivity increased more than 10 percent, and turnover declined nearly 70 percent.

In a second case, a pharmaceutical company replaced coffee makers used by a few marketing workers with a larger cafe area. The result? Increased sales and less turnover. A third example is from a tech company. The workers who sat at larger tables in the cafeteria, thus communicating more, were found to be more productive than workers who sat at smaller tables.[ix]

Adam Grant, an organizational psychologist, presents a fourth example company that facilitates communication in his book, *Give and Take: A Revolutionary Approach to Success*. Grant describes a large telecommunications firm in San Francisco. The professional engineers who worked at the firm were asked to rate themselves and each other on how much time they spent giving and receiving information from one another. The results reinforce the connection between communication and productivity. The engineers who gave the most help were the most productive and were held in the highest respect by their peers. By giving often, engineers built up more trust and attracted more cooperation from across their work groups, not just from the people they helped.[x]

In his book, Grant also tells how a former CEO at Deloitte improved his communication style. The executive, Jim Quigley, set a goal in meetings to talk no more than 20 percent of the time. "One of my objectives is listening. Many times you can have bigger impact if you know what to ask, rather than knowing what to say," Quigley explained. As he increased his questions, Quigley found himself gaining a deeper understanding of other people's needs.[xi]

As you can see from these examples, simple steps such as arranging the work environment to facilitate communication and encouraging people to interact informally pay big dividends. Talking, listening, and asking questions are learning experiences. Enjoyable learning experiences. The more you learn about your people and the more they learn about each other, the easier it is for everyone to work together toward a common goal. That's the key to managerial success.

Talking, listening, and asking questions are learning experiences.

Summary

This chapter presents a model that is the framework for the book's premise. Beginning with the two cornerstones of diversity appreciation and cultural competence, the chapter shows that managerial communication should be frequent, open, and honest. Frequent, respectful interactions with peers, bosses, subordinates, and other stakeholders will result in stronger work relationships. These relationships, in turn, will foster the key emotional conditions of trust, loyalty, commitment, and job satisfaction. People feeling these emotions are engaged in their work. They are motivated to work cooperatively, which leads to productivity and organizational success. Managers who understand this sequence will be able to get along, get it done, and get ahead.

Endnotes

    i. L. McWorthy, D.D. Henningsen (2014). "Looking at Favorable and Unfavorable Superior-Subordinate Relationships through Dominance and Affiliation Lenses," *International Journal of Business Communication* 51, no. 2, pp. 123–37.
   ii. M. Shafiq, M. Zia-ur-Rehman, M. Rashid (2013). "Impact of Compensation, Training and Development and Supervisory Support on Organizational Commitment," *Compensation and Benefits Review* 45, no. 5, pp. 278–85.
  iii. O. Hargie, D. Tourish, N. Wilson (2001). "Communication Audits and the Effects of Increased Information: A Follow-Up Study,"

Journal of Business Communication 39, no. 4, pp. 414–36. See also G.F. Thomas, R. Zolin, J.L. Hartman (2009). "The Central Role of Communication in Developing Trust and Its Effect on Employee Involvement," *Journal of Business Communication* 46, no. 3, pp. 287–310.

iv. Project Management Institute, Inc. (2013). "The High Cost of Low Performance: The Essential Role of Communications" (Pulse of the Profession In-depth Report), Retrieved from www.pmi.org

v. T. Schwartz, C. Porath (2014, June 1). "Why You Hate Work," *New York Times*, p. 1SR.

vi. Ibid.

vii. A.B. Carroll (2006, July 29). "Trust is the Key When Rating Great Workplaces," Retrieved from http://onlineathens.com/stories/073006/business_20060730047.shtml, p. 1.

viii. K. Mishra, L. Boynton, A. Mishra (2014). "Driving Employee Engagement: the Expanded Role of Internal Communications," *International Journal of Business Communication* 51, no. 2, pp. 183–202.

ix. S. Lohr (2014, June 21). "Unblinking Eyes Track Employees: Workplace Surveillance Sees Good and Bad," *New York Times,* Retrieved from http://www.nytimes.com/2014/06/22/technology/workplace-surveillance-sees-good-and-bad.html?_r=0

x. A. Grant (2013). *Give and Take: A Revolutionary Approach to Success* (New York, NY: Viking Press), pp. 58–9.

xi. A. Grant, p. 265.

PART 2

Get Along

CHAPTER 4

Strategies for Finding Out What's Going On

As discussed in Part One of this book, the daily interactions that you engage in upward, downward, laterally, and diagonally along the organizational hierarchy will determine your success. The Sequence for Success model (Figure 4.1) shows that interpersonal communication is the first step in the sequence that culminates in organizational success. That's because communication leads to relationships; relationships foster important emotional conditions such as loyalty, job satisfaction, and commitment; and in turn, these emotional conditions trigger effective work performance. The more people engage in an organization's life, the more connected they become and the more effective the organization becomes. The communication strategies for "getting along" will enable you to "get it done" and ultimately to "get ahead."

Part Two focuses on the daily conversational behaviors that will help you get along with coworkers, subordinates, and bosses. This chapter describes a range of communication strategies that will keep you informed about the people and events in your work environment. Chapter 5 describes communication strategies that will build stronger work relationships. The relationship level is where most of the work gets done. It's also where you experience most of the difficulties.

A key concept in the relationship process is the notion of emotional intelligence (EI). The next section explains this concept and its relevance.

Emotional Intelligence

How good are you at staying calm under pressure at work? When others complain to you, do you show empathy even though deep down you may feel that they are just whining? Do your coworkers think you are easy to get along with? Is it easy to socialize with your team?

Figure 4.1 The Sequence for Success Model

Such behaviors reflect social and emotional competence. Popularly known as EI, social and emotional competence has been shown to be a better predictor of professional success than cognitive intelligence or specialized knowledge.[i] In fact, research shows that EI accounts for an amazing 58 percent of performance in all job types. Furthermore, 90 percent of high job performers are also high in EI, yet only 20 percent of low job performers are high in EI.

Emotional intelligence is the ability to recognize, understand, and respond to emotions in ourselves and others.

Research focusing on business leaders shows that EI scores are the highest for middle managers but lowest for executives. In trying to explain that difference, the researchers observed that executives are more likely to be promoted because of what they know or how long they have worked, rather than for their management skills or social awareness. However, high EI executives are the best performers.[ii]

Briefly, EI is defined as the ability to recognize, understand, and respond to emotions in ourselves and others. Unlike personality, which remains stable throughout most of our lives, EI can be improved with training. By improving our ability to recognize and understand emotions, we can do a much better job of managing our behavior and our social interactions.[iii] Daniel Goleman's landmark book about EI lists six ways people can cope with workplace pressures and the resulting stress on relationships. These competencies are generally accepted as the starting point for emotion management. They include the ability to:

1. Become self-aware in managing emotions and controlling impulses
2. Set goals and perform well
3. Be motivated and creative
4. Empathize with others
5. Handle relationships effectively
6. Develop appropriate social skills[iv]

Mastering these competencies will greatly affect the way you interact with coworkers, subordinates, and bosses.

In their book, *Emotional Intelligence 2.0*, Bradberry and Greaves offer many practical suggestions for improving your self-awareness, managing yourself, becoming more socially aware, and managing relationships in all aspects of life. Here are some highlights that apply to workplace relationships:

1. During meetings, use people's names. Don't take too many notes, but use nonverbal behaviors (looking, nodding) to indicate that you are paying attention as you listen.

2. When interacting with culturally diverse people, be open, be respectful, be sincere, and be curious.

3. During disagreements, acknowledge the other person's point or feelings before stating your own opinion. Be willing to offer a "fix it" statement no matter who is right.

4. When interacting with lower status employees, use compliments liberally, and always be pleasant and courteous.

5. Have tough conversations instead of letting problems fester.

6. When things explode, under-react until you have learned more.

7. Get real value out of every social interaction, even with people you don't like.

Social and emotional competence will smooth your everyday interactions on the job. That's how you'll be able to stay in the loop. Next, we take a closer look at vertical interactions—those between you and your subordinates. "That seems easy enough," you may be thinking. "I tell them what they need to know, and they tell me what I need to know." Well, maybe it is easy to share information when it's neutral or positive. But conversations are tougher between you and your subordinates when expressing differences and when bad news is involved. Are your conversations about negative topics a matter of, "I tell them what they need to know, and they tell me what they think I want to hear"? If so, read on.

Giving Bad News to Subordinates

A typical tough conversation is the one in which you must give subordinates information they don't want to hear. Any change in policy or procedure is generally unwelcome simply because it is a change. Employees are comfortable with the status quo, despite the tendency to complain about the way things are. When an impending change in policy or procedure will result in negative situations—layoffs, reductions in compensation, relocation, increases in workload, elimination of breaks or downtime—it's even more important to know how to announce the bad news without damaging the work relationship. The worst that can happen at this point is that the communication channel in your functional area closes up.

To keep the lines of communication open so you continue to know what's going on in bad times, follow these steps:

Format for a bad news message

- Buffer
- Reasons
- Bad news
- Goodwill

1. Begin with a buffer. Typical buffers are a compliment ("Good job with that angry client yesterday, Ben"), statement of appreciation ("Thanks for taking my call"), agreement on a principle ("Safety is our top priority"), or a shared goal ("We're out to bury Eldridge"). This establishes a positive, or at least neutral, connection.
2. Give reasons for the upcoming change. Presenting background information, facts and incidents, will help your people understand what's behind the decision.
3. Deliver the bad news. By now the employees are prepared. They won't like what they hear, but they'll know why they are hearing it. Stick to the facts as you know them. Avoid sharing your doubts and other negative emotions, because feelings are contagious and your people will take their cue from you.
4. End with goodwill. Express confidence in their ability to weather the change and reassure them that you'll remain at their side, supporting and keeping them informed throughout the transition.

Receiving Bad News from Subordinates

If you're like most bosses, you're probably insulated from the truth. When you ask your subordinates how they are, they say, "Fine." "Things are going great." So how do you find out what's really going on and what you need to fix?

One strategy is the "Triple Two." Ask your subordinates what two things you should stop doing, two things you should start doing, and two things you need to keep doing. That gives your people permission to speak freely. Asking for honest feedback makes it easier for your direct reports to go beyond what they think you want to hear.[v] The Triple Two also works when you want to repair strained relationships with colleagues and coworkers who you think might be withholding important information.

Of course, it's important that you be authentic about asking subordinates to give you the straight talk. If you punish them for telling you something you don't want to hear or fail to act on any of their input, they will stop telling you anything. And that's a recipe for failure. The next paragraphs offer suggestions for ways to respond to subordinates' feedback. We begin with saying sorry.

Apologizing

When you have messed up and your subordinates want you to make amends, there's a right way and a wrong way to apologize. The wrong way is to use the word, "but." "I'm sorry I hurt your feelings, but …" denies wrongdoing. It also indicates that you aren't really apologizing. Instead, to diffuse anger and resentment, try the "MIDAS" strategy:

M = admit you made a **M**istake
I = admit you caused **I**njury
D = explain what you'll **D**o differently
A = say how you'll make **A**mends
S = Stop talking[vi]

Research shows that in many situations, the "M" and the "I" count more than the "D" with the people you offended. That is, they might not expect you to—or even want you to—do anything differently. They simply want you to admit wrongdoing. Much of the research on the effects of apologies has focused on the health care profession. In the past, medical professionals were reluctant to apologize to patients for fear that it would be interpreted as admitting fault, which would open them up to malpractice suits. Similarly, in business settings, corporate legal counsel has often urged against apologies because of the link to liability and the threat of lawsuits. Surprisingly, however, medical professionals who apologized have actually seen *lower* rates of malpractice claims.

Nonverbally, when apologizing, be sure to use the gestures, posture, and eye contact that you would like the offended person to use. If you behave positively and calmly, you will influence the other person's reaction.

Cultural Differences in Responding to Feedback

Not everything your subordinates tell you requires an apology. But they do expect some sort of response. As we discussed in Part One of this book, trusting relationships are built on continuous communication, on two-way interactions. Therefore, when you ask what's going on and they tell you, you are usually expected to respond.

Your first response to bad news may be denial or defense. It's natural to react negatively to negative information, especially when you feel threatened. But as a manager, showing empathy in bad news situations will go far to create and maintain open channels. Once empathy is established, you can move on to an exploration of solutions. Sometimes subordinates don't have solutions, but in a surprising number of situations, they do, and it's wise to listen to them.

Culture can affect the exchange of feelings and ideas, problems, and solutions. Various cultures view feedback differently. For example, in the United States and Europe, workers prefer direct communication and expect honest feedback. In Asian cultures, on the other hand, workers prefer communicating more indirectly, and they may prefer feedback to be subtle rather than blunt. In Asian cultures, silence is respected. Silence, rather than talk, communicates. As a result, when working with people from Asian cultures, managers can benefit from learning to use silence as a type of response.[vii] Even if you "know for sure" what someone is going to say, be patient and let him complete his thoughts. Rather than assuming, an open attitude will help you see the other person's side of a situation and strengthen the working relationship.

Strategies for Checking Understanding

An inappropriate reaction will shut the channel immediately when you're on the receiving end of the communication channel between you and your subordinates. This section presents three strategies for keeping the channel open, so you can stay informed. The strategies are listening, reading nonverbals, and asking questions. These three strategies are especially critical when the information coming your way is negative. Applying the strategies also will strengthen your rapport with the speaker.

Listening

As a business professional, you probably spend half to two-thirds of your time listening, yet 75 to 90 percent of what you hear is ignored, misunderstood, or forgotten.[viii] That's because listening is hard work. It's not a passive experience. Your brain is not a sponge that absorbs whatever comes along. Listening is also difficult when you're busy and distracted with work. Your brain can think at least four times faster than anyone can talk, so while you're waiting for someone to get to the point, you've mentally moved on.

Listening requires active participation in the conversation. To create a healthy work atmosphere you have to keep the communication channel open. Begin by preparing yourself—both physically and psychologically—to listen.

1. Pick the best possible place. While it is not always possible to change the place, don't overlook better facilities when available. Selecting the best place helps reduce internal and external noise.

2. Pick the best possible time. As with place, it is not always possible to change the time. However, because time influences the psychological barriers of motivation, emotion, and willingness, deciding when to meet may significantly alter the conversation's outcome.

3. Think about personal biases that may be present. If you are unaware of personal bias, you may become selective and hear only what you want to hear. Emotional words can also trigger listener bias. Such phrases as "typical humorless accountant," "we tried that before, and it didn't work," or "all engineers think alike" can lead to emotional responses. The danger in such phrases is that they cause a listener to pay attention only to certain parts of a message. Don't let bias distract you from understanding the message.

Interesting research shows that men and women have different listening styles. When women listen, they tend to focus on the relationship.

When they process information, their goal is to zoom in on emotions and mood. In an effort to relay support, women are willing to allow others to open up and reveal what they care about. By contrast, men tend to listen for facts and information and are less comfortable handling emotional content. They are interested in power and control, and they listen for solutions rather than for empathy.[ix]

In interactive listening situations, you are expected not only to receive but also to respond to what the other person has said. An easy-to-remember formula for an effective response is ACE—Affirm, Comment, Expand.

Respond with the ACE Formula:

1. Affirm
2. Comment
3. Expand

Begin your response by *affirming* what you have heard the other person say. You accomplish this with a paraphrase, which reflects her meaning as you understood it rather than her exact words. After proving that you got the message, you can *comment* on it by saying whether you agree or disagree. Next you *expand* by explaining why you agree or disagree, adding your own two cents to the discussion. Following the ACE formula will lower any barriers and encourage the other person to be receptive and open to your opinions and ideas.

Reading Nonverbals

The old saying that a picture speaks a thousand words is still true. How you look and how you sound contribute more to the impression you create than what you say. Therefore, when your coworkers, bosses, and subordinates are sending messages, it's important to show attention with your whole body, not just your words.

Similarly, whenever you send messages to others at work, the receivers will be reading your nonverbals. They will judge you on two dimensions: *competence* and *warmth*. Competence gets to how smart, able, and skilled your receivers think you are. Warmth is about how nice, engaging, and friendly they think you are. Obviously, for maximum success in communication, the goal is to demonstrate competence and warmth through your nonverbal behavior. The problem is that, typically, as confidence goes up, warmth goes down, especially for women in business.

Here are some easy-to-adopt behaviors that will help you project both competence and warmth nonverbally, whether you are speaking or listening. First, practice eye contact with everyone in the room. Avoid sweeping back and forth with your eyes like a windshield wiper, but instead hold eye contact with each person for a few seconds. Be mindful that eye contact patterns are different for speaking and for listening—in the United States, listeners look more than speakers do. Eye contact also differs from culture to culture—for instance, the Japanese are generally less comfortable with extended eye contact than are Americans. Other nonverbal signals are also important to the attitude we convey, though their interpretation and impact also vary across cultures.

Nonverbal expressions of competence and warmth:

- Eye contact
- Hand gestures
- Head tilt
- Posture and distance

A second nonverbal technique to build the impression of competence and warmth is to keep your hands in front of your torso, elbows bent, and palms up. This pose allows you to gesture easily when speaking to reinforce your words. Avoid pointing at people, which is considered aggressive and dominant in many cultures. Keeping your hands open rather than clutching a pen, fiddling with a paper clip, or tenting your fingers, looks relaxed and receptive.

Third, be aware of how you hold your head. Tilting it makes you seem attentive, especially when combined with eye contact. Nodding your head as you listen can encourage the other person to continue speaking. However, constant nodding looks habitual and can work against your intended impression. Be aware that some cultures interpret a nod to mean "I agree," not just "I'm listening." In addition, there are gender differences in the use of this nonverbal behavior, with women tilting and nodding more than men do as they listen.

A fourth nonverbal technique is to maintain a posture that makes you look involved, alert, and open. Whether standing or sitting, keep your body relaxed, leaning slightly in as you listen and speak. The distance you are expected to maintain during conversation varies from culture to culture. In the U.S. business environment, "social distance" is typically 3 to 5 feet. Getting within arm's reach is considered "intimate"; it can also be interpreted as aggressive and asserting power or authority. On the other hand, staying 5 feet apart is considered "public," too formal for interaction in small groups. Be sensitive to cultural preferences when seeking a comfortable distance.

Asking Questions

So far, we've examined two strategies for checking understanding—listening and reading nonverbals. A third strategy that will help you when you're trying to understand a message is to ask good questions. The type of answer you get will largely depend on the type of question you ask (see Table 4.1).

An *open-ended* question calls for a long answer. It is designed to open the door and get the other person talking. Typically it begins with "why," "what," "how," or "tell me about." You usually use open-ended questions at the beginning of a conversation.

A *closed-ended* question calls for a one-word answer such as a fact, a number, a date, a "yes" or "no." Typically it begins with "when," "how often," "how many," or "did you." You usually use closed-ended questions during a conversation to pin down information and seek commitment.

Table 4.1 Types of Questions

Question Type	Use	Example
Open	Get information Get the other person talking	What happened? What are you worried about?
Closed	Get commitment Get facts and details	Will you do that? When did that happen?
Probe	Get elaboration Get clarification	What happened after that? Was that before or after he called?
Directed	Get agreement	That was a mistake, wasn't it?

A *probe* is a secondary or follow-up question. It can be open or closed. When you want the speaker to elaborate, ask an open probe such as "And then what did she do?" When you want the speaker to provide clarification, ask a closed probe such as "How often has she done that?"

A *directed* question is a leading question. Typically, it begins with a statement and then calls for agreement. An example is, "You won't be late for work again, will you?" Use a directed question toward the end of a conversation, when you are seeking consensus.

Listening to the Grapevine

Our discussion of listening has emphasized formal speaking–listening situations at work. However, informal, casual listening can also be extremely important. As a manager, you should always be aware of the rumors that circulate on the grapevine. At times, these rumors can provide important information; at other times, it may be important to change the rumors; and sometimes it's best to ignore the rumors. But always stay tuned in.

What causes rumors in contemporary workplaces? To answer this question, the following formula is helpful:

Rumors = Ambiguity × Interest

Rumors are created when the situation is ambiguous. If all information were available and clear from the formal channels, no rumors would be created. When the situation is ambiguous and also interesting, rumors will fly. This relationship has an important implication for managers. By paying attention to the grapevine, you can determine what is interesting to your employees.

Research indicates that information on the grapevine in organizations is 70 to 90 percent accurate. However, some amount of distortion always exists.[x] This core of truth along with the degree of distortion is often what makes a message on the grapevine believable, interesting, and durable.

As information moves from person to person on the grapevine, it tends to undergo three kinds of change. The first change is *leveling*, where details are dropped or simplified. This process is especially prevalent when the rumor is extremely complex. The second kind of change is *sharpening*, where people add drama and vivid details. Employees work to make a story better and more entertaining as they pass it along. The third change is *assimilating*, the tendency of people to adjust or modify rumors, to mold them to fit their personal needs. This makes the rumor more useful to those feeding the grapevine.[xi]

In listening effectively to informal communication, you need to determine the extent to which leveling, sharpening, and assimilating have occurred. Inaccurate rumors can sometimes call for action. Let's say you work in a manufacturing environment, and rumors are flying about a massive layoff because of the new machinery being installed. If you hear these incorrect rumors, you can't ignore them. Members of the management team should meet formally with employees to assure them no lay-offs will occur and that the new equipment will offer significant benefits. Listening to rumors will help you to prevent losses in employee morale. As one manager once said to me, "It's important to listen to the talk on the street."

Employees prefer to get their information from the formal channels, but they turn to informal channels when the formal have dried up because no one can work in a vacuum. Managers concerned about rampant rumors should keep in mind the relationship between formal and informal channels.

Summary

"Getting along" begins with knowing yourself and managing yourself. Once you have gained competency in self-awareness and self-management, you can become competent in social awareness and be able to manage relationships for maximum outcomes.

The goal is to stay informed about what's going on around you. To do that, you must nurture the communication channels between you and your subordinates, peers, and bosses. To check how well you understand what's going on, listen, read nonverbals, and ask questions. You can use the strategies presented in this chapter for keeping information flowing in formal and informal channels. An informed manager is a high-performing manager.

Endnotes

i. L.S. Sigmar, G.E. Hynes, K.L. Hill (2012). "Strategies for Teaching Social and Emotional Intelligence in Business Communication," *Business Communication Quarterly* 75, no. 3, pp. 301–17.

ii. D. Ryback (2012). *Putting Emotional Intelligence to Work* (New York, NY: Routledge).

iii. T. Bradberry, J. Greaves (2009). *Emotional Intelligence 2.0* (San Diego, CA: Talent Smart).

iv. D. Goleman (1995). *Emotional Intelligence* (New York, NY: Bantam Publishing Co.).

v. I.M. Sixel (2013, May 16). "Permission to Speak Freely to the Boss," *Houston Chronicle*, 2013, p. D1.

vi. Ibid.

vii. W.B. Gudykunst (1998). *Bridging Differences: Effective Intergroup Communication*, 3rd ed. (Thousand Oaks, CA: Sage Publications)., pp. 173–74.

viii. M. Munter (2012). *Guide to Managerial Communication: Effective Business Writing and Speaking*, 9th ed. (Upper Saddle River, NJ: Prentice Hall), p. 154.

ix. J.T. Wood (2013). *Gendered Lives: Communication, Gender, and Culture,* 10th ed. (Boston: Wadsworth), p. 127.

x. H.B. Vickery (1984, January). "Tapping into the Employee Grapevine," *Association Management,* pp. 59–64.

xi. P.V. Lewis (1987). *Organizational Communication: The Essence of Effective Management,* 3rd ed. (New York, NY: Wiley & Sons), pp. 46–48.

CHAPTER 5

Strategies for Strengthening Work Relationships

"Getting along" on the job means developing and maintaining strong work relationships. In the previous chapter, we saw that relationships are built on communication—if there is no communication, there is no relationship. Think of someone you see around your worksite from time to time but you haven't ever talked with. Do you have a relationship with that person? No. Now think of someone at work that you do engage with—a boss, a subordinate, or a peer. Do you have a relationship with that person? Yes, of course. Whether the relationship is negative or positive, whether you like or dislike that person, your relationship is the result of interpersonal communication.

Chapter 4 described a number of strategies for finding out what's going on in your work environment. These strategies for listening, checking understanding, and responding are invaluable communication competencies. As the Sequence for Success model (Figure 5.1) shows, interpersonal communication leads to interpersonal relationships.

Now that we have explored the connection between communication competence and interpersonal relationships, we are ready to move further along the Sequence for Success and explore the connection between interpersonal relationships and several other important elements—loyalty, commitment, job satisfaction, and trust. When those emotional conditions are present, people are more productive because they can work together more smoothly. In Part Three of this book we will describe how "getting along" leads to "getting it done."

Figure 5.1 Sequence for Success

The New Golden Rule

As a child, you probably were taught to "do unto others as you would have them do unto you." This maxim is based on the ethic of reciprocity, and its roots can be traced back over 4,000 years. Variations of the Golden Rule are found in writings from ancient Egypt, Greece, China, and other cultures, as well as all major religions of the world.

In the workplace, it makes some sense to treat others as you would like to be treated. However, as a manager, you need to do better. When building relationships, try treating others as *they* want to be treated, not the way *you* want to be treated. Sharon Sloane, CEO of Will Interactive, a maker of training videos, calls this version of the Golden Rule the "Platinum Rule: Do unto others as they would have you do unto them."[i] She explains that this ethic recognizes that not everybody is motivated by the same thing that motivates you. In short, leaders should figure out what makes their people tick.

> New Golden Rule: Treat others as they want to be treated, not the way you want to be treated.

Managing by the new Golden Rule starts with using your communication competencies to learn about your people and what's going on with them, then building a relationship based on that knowledge. Briefly, the strategies introduced in Chapter 4 that will help you understand people at work are:

1. Observe their verbal and nonverbal behavior
2. Ask questions to test the accuracy of your observations
3. Walk in their shoes to gain understanding and empathy

Ask yourself, "If I were this person, how would I feel? What would I say? How would I react?" Developing empathy is particularly important—and difficult—in a culturally diverse workplace. However, conflict management, decision making, problem solving, and other leadership activities are much easier and more effective when "dynamic connectedness" among workers is present.[ii] No longer do people work alone; 100 percent of the Fortune 500 companies and 90 percent of all U.S. companies implement some form of group decision process. Teamwork demands strong interdependent relationships.

Empathy

Having close relationships with colleagues—even just one—makes a difference in personal and organizational growth. Bridges are built across cultural divides one person at a time. Researchers at the University of

Chicago provide evidence for this claim. They studied hundreds of teenagers from cultures that are historically in conflict (Israelis and Palestinians, Catholics and Protestants in Northern Ireland, rural whites and urban blacks in the United States). For several years the Seeds for Peace program has brought teenagers together for a three-week summer camp in Maine, sleeping, eating, playing games, and participating in discussions. The University of Chicago researchers measured how the relationships that the students developed with each other changed their attitudes.

The results are striking. Regardless of their initial attitudes, the teens who formed just one close relationship with someone from the other group were the ones who developed the most positive attitudes toward the other group. The conclusion is that forming just one friendship was as good or better a predictor of future attitudes toward the conflicting group than the total number of friendships that a person formed.[iii]

> Creating opportunities for coworkers and subordinates to interact informally fosters empathy.

As a manager, you can foster the development of empathy among your subordinates by forming them into teams or workgroups and assigning them a project. The proximity and forced interaction will pave the way toward empathic relationships. That's because the group members will have to find common ground. Further, as the employees engage with each other, they will become more emotionally invested in the organization. Ultimately, the organization will become smarter and more effective because the work of the organization is done through person-to-person relationships.

These strategies apply to horizontal as well as vertical work relationships. Just as you can influence subordinates to develop empathy, there are ways to encourage empathy among your coworkers. For instance, you can gather everyone to celebrate an achievement, a holiday, or even a birthday. That will give everyone an opportunity to exchange perceptions and learn about each other in a low-stress environment. Informal, face-to-face interactions work best for developing empathy because both verbal and nonverbal cues are exchanged; the combination gives a more complete understanding of the information being shared.

"Lean" communication channels such as virtual meetings, text messages, and email exchanges are a poor substitute for face-to-face interactions. If your people are scattered in the field or telecommuting from remote locations, it's much more difficult for them to develop empathic relationships. Be creative and try to get everyone together from time to time. The benefits will be worth the cost.

Loyalty, Commitment, and Job Satisfaction

A study by the Great Place to Work Institute found that employees enjoy working where they "trust the people they work for, have pride in what they do, and enjoy the people they work with."[iv] Open, two-way communication is a hallmark of such workplaces.

Employee loyalty and commitment to an organization increase when they "feel a strong emotional bond to their employer, recommending it to others and committing time and effort to help the organization succeed."[v] Committed employees have been linked to important organizational outcomes such as higher retention, fewer safety violations, reduced absenteeism, and perhaps most importantly, higher productivity.[vi]

Supervisory communication has consistently been identified as a key factor in employee commitment. As discussed in Chapter 4, honest, frequent communication keeps workers informed about the organization's goals and how they can contribute to reaching the goals. One company I worked with found that the need for periodic employee meetings with the CEO became unnecessary when they built communication into the culture of their organization. As routine communication improved, attendance at the meetings with the CEO dwindled to nothing. "We already know what's going on" was the employees' explanation.

An additional benefit of consistent, honest, and frequent communication is that it makes workers feel appreciated and respected. When employees believe their supervisor supports them, they respond by becoming more committed and engaged in their job. Engaged employees have a strong, positive relationship with their supervisor. Putting it another way, employees don't quit their job, they quit their boss.

Employees don't quit their job, they quit their boss.

Employee engagement has become a major theme in current management literature. In a recent Gallup poll, a startling 70 percent of American workers said they were not engaged with their jobs, or were actively disengaged. When asked why, the workers complained about the lack of opportunity for self-expression, personal growth, and meaningful work. Finding meaning is about being engaged. It's about feeling important, feeling recognized, and feeling informed.

Employee engagement levels are down all across the United States, but they appear to be particularly weak among Millennials. In a 2011 Harris Interactive report commissioned by the Career Advisory Board, "meaning" was the top career priority for those between the ages of 21 and 31. If you are from a previous generation, like me, you are more likely to value loyalty to the company above meaningful work. You may even be willing to admit that you've complained about younger employees' lack of commitment to their organization. But it's risky for managers to ignore such generational differences in priorities, whether real or imagined, because they may affect morale, retention, and even productivity.

The single best tool to enhance engagement is face-to-face, one-to-one communication between you and your subordinate. As a manager, you can increase your employees' level of engagement by making small but key changes in your daily workplace interactions. You can talk to your people more often than emailing them. You can notice their contributions more often than their mistakes. You can simply ask your employees whether they had a good day and what moments made it so.[vii] Then listen. Try to adjust the work environment to make those moments happen more frequently.

To keep your workers from going elsewhere, find out why they are unhappy. To keep your workers happy, find out why they stay. Conducting an exit survey may reveal the working conditions—or people—that drove someone away, but it's too late at that point to impact the leaver's attitudes. Instead, conduct a retention survey among current employees. A retention survey can make people feel valued and will determine what the company can do to improve employee satisfaction, whether it's training, benefits, improved communication channels, or recognition programs. Sometimes you can even redesign the individual's job to make it more closely align with personal strengths and passions.

An engaged workforce is a happier workforce and a more productive workforce.

For maximum impact, responsibility for employee engagement should be corporate wide. Indeed, in the best companies, a culture of open communication begins with the CEO and other top executives, who know that employees must be engaged so they will contribute to the company's goals. Internal communication processes are in place in these companies to ensure that employees understand the company's mission and how they fit into it.

Companies with an open communication culture invest in a range of platforms to support employee dialogue and promote engagement. Meetings, web casts, executive presentations, newsletters, feedback mechanisms, forums, company blogs, and other interactive media are examples of formal internal channels designed to build engagement. As a vice president of an energy company said, "The more employees understand and feel like they're contributing or in line with the company strategy, the more productive they are and the higher the morale and [the] lower [the] turnover."[viii]

Trust

Putting your employees first, helping them to feel engaged and committed, is a matter of trust above all else. Employees who are not engaged in what they do don't trust their supervisors or their companies. Today's employees are looking for a place where they can do their best work. They are looking for cultural fit and trusting relationships on the job.

Trusting Them

If you want your employees to trust you, then you must trust them. Remember Sharon Sloane, CEO of Will Interactive? Here's the extent to which she trusts her people:

> "We give what we call mission-type orders here. I will be very clear with what the goal is, what the objective is. Then I'm basically going to give you the latitude to do it. If you need my help or have a problem, come see me. Otherwise, I bless you."[ix]

Trusting your employees means nurturing their independence, allowing workers freedom to express their opinions and follow preferred work styles without denying those of others. This willingness to let people approach the work their preferred way—so long as the goal is achieved—is particularly important if you have a culturally diverse workforce. Diverse environments call for a high tolerance for disagreement. Ask yourself, "Which is more important—that things get done my way, or that things get done?"

A healthy work climate is a trusting climate. Douglas McGregor, a famous expert in organizational communication, summarized the optimal characteristics of a work climate:

1. The atmosphere is informal, relaxed, and comfortable.
2. Everyone participates in discussion about the work at hand.
3. Everyone is committed to the task and the objective.
4. Everyone listens to each other. Every idea is given a fair hearing.
5. Disagreement is not suppressed. Rather than silencing dissent, the reasons are examined, and the group seeks rational solutions.
6. Important decisions are reached by consensus.
7. Criticism is frequent, frank, and relatively comfortable, but not personal.
8. People freely express their feelings.
9. The leader does not dominate.
10. The group monitors itself.[x]

Do these characteristics sound like the characteristics of your work group? If you are comfortable hearing differences expressed, if you trust people to find their own way to reach the performance goal, the result will be relational satisfaction, commitment to excellence, and organizational success.

Trusting You

Of course, if you want your employees to trust you, you need to be trustworthy, yourself. The following paragraphs present ways to develop trust. Briefly, trust is developed when:

1. Your words, nonverbals, and actions are consistent.
2. Your behaviors are predictable.
3. You explain what is going on and why (transparency).

Elements of trust:

- Consistency
- Predictability
- Transparency

Let's take a closer look at these factors. First, make your words, non-verbals, and actions consistent. As you read in Chapter 4, when what you say is inconsistent with how you look and sound, people believe how you look and sound. If you say, "These procedural changes are going to be an improvement," while looking glum, your people won't believe the changes will be beneficial, and they will resist adopting them.

Appropriate nonverbal behaviors for managers can be summarized as those demonstrating a confident manner. Confidence builds trust. Stand and sit straight, keep your head balanced on your neck, and be aware of eye contact patterns. Use a clear, pleasant but strong tone of voice and minimize disfluencies ("uh," "um," "you know," "like").

Appropriate verbal behaviors for managers who want to build trust include using inclusive words to indicate that both you and your listeners belong to a group. Words such as "we," "us," and "our" rather than "I" and "my" signal a social category that will increase loyalty and trust for members of the in-group. Another verbal tool is to disclose more frequently, sharing information as much and as often as you can. This will reduce uncertainty and increase trust, even if your people won't like what they hear. Telling people more about what's going on will also increase predictability. A third verbal tool is to use concrete language—facts and words with clear meanings—rather than abstract or vague terms. Speaking conceptually or with lofty, vague expressions causes doubt and distrust.

Trustworthy talk is:

- Inclusive
- Frequent
- Complete
- Concrete

Finally, trustworthy talk is honest. The 2012 Edelman Trust Barometer calls for companies to "practice radical transparency," which means telling employees the truth about what's going on.[xi] If a company shares information, employees feel a sense of belonging and a part of a shared mission. This develops a bond of trust between employees and the company. Leaders who are transparent, who openly share truthful information with their people, retain credibility.

Cultural Differences and Work Relationships

So far, we have focused on ways to strengthen work relationships in a democratic, egalitarian culture. However, the contemporary work environment requires recognizing that there are significant differences in what people of other cultures think are appropriate supervisor–subordinate and peer relationships.

Cultures that value authoritarian leadership reward managers who are directive, prescriptive, and judgmental. The boss's word is not to be questioned. Subordinates are expected to be dependent and submissive, suppressing their opinions. An example of such a culture is Korea. In his best-selling book, *Outliers*, Malcolm Gladwell described Korean national airlines as once having the worst accident record of all. Careful investigation of the reasons for the alarming frequency of plane crashes revealed that the crashes were often due to pilot error. Apparently even when crew members perceived their captain making mistakes, they didn't try to correct the captain, because they believed it was not their place to question authority. Once training programs incorporated the notion that calling attention to potential errors was a crewmember's duty, the airline's record of accidents improved significantly.

In authoritarian cultures where leaders are expected to be dominant (and some U.S. companies are still like that), the strategies emphasized in this chapter will fail, and managers who apply them will be considered weak. For example, companies in Spain and Portugal are more likely to stress the importance of interpersonal communication and employee satisfaction than are companies in Germany and France.

Generational differences regarding the importance of solid workplace relationships have also been noted. While stereotyping is risky because it doesn't account for individual differences, there is ample evidence that many Boomers are loyal to their employers and exhibit long-term commitment, to the point of refusing to retire when eligible. Gen-Xers are known to be more individualistic, skeptical of authority, and think of themselves as free agents; they seek more work-life balance than their workaholic parents do. Millennials are reputed to feel special, entitled, and approval seeking; they are group-oriented and achievement-motivated, but they will leave employment if they feel unappreciated.[xii]

To become a culturally sensitive manager, you need to assess your employees' personal achievement needs and relationship expectations and create a work environment that maximizes everyone's comfort level. Look for possible cultural, generational, even gender-based differences among your coworkers and subordinates that might influence the development of work relationships. If you're not sure about the implications of what you are observing, ask questions. The goal is to gain communication competence across contexts.

Summary

Getting along at work involves building and maintaining relationships. This chapter presents a range of communication strategies that will strengthen relationships among workers and between workers and their managers so they can "get along." First, the new Golden Rule is to treat others as they want to be treated. Foster dynamic connectedness by creating opportunities for formal and informal get-togethers so workers can form empathic relationships.

Loyalty, commitment, and job satisfaction will grow when employees feel engaged in meaningful work. Trust will develop when managers are consistent and predictable in their verbal and nonverbal behavior. Communication that is frequent, true, and comprehensive will also contribute to trustworthiness.

Managers should be sensitive to differing perceptions of the importance of work relationships and interpersonal communication among cultures, generations, and genders.

Endnotes

i. A. Bryant (2014, August 3). "See Yourself as Others See You: Interview with Sharon Sloane," *New York Times*, p. 2.

ii. P.M. Sias, K.J. Krone, F.M. Jablin (2002). "An Ecological Systems Perspective on Workplace Relationships," in *Handbook of Interpersonal Communication*, 3rd ed., eds. M.L. Knapp, J.A. Daly (Thousand Oaks, CA: Sage Publications), pp. 615–42.

iii. J. Schroeder, J.L. Risen (2014, July 28). "Befriending the Enemy: Outgroup Friendship Longitudinally Predicts Intergroup Attitudes in a Coexistence Program for Israelis and Palestinians," *Group Processes and Intergroup Relations Journal*, doi: 10.1177/1368430214542257.

iv. A.B. Carroll (2006, July 29). "Trust is the Key When Rating Great Workplaces," Retrieved from http://onlineathens.com/stories/073006/business_20060730047.shtml, p. 1.

v. B. Quirk (2008). *Making the Connections: Using Internal Communication To Turn Strategy Into Action* (Burlington, VT: Gower), p. 102.

vi. J. Robison (2012, January 5). "Boosting Engagement at Stryker," *Gallup Management Journal*, Retrieved from http://gmj.gallup.com/content/150956/Boosting-Engagement-Stryker.aspx, p. 1.

vii. A. Hurst (2014, April 20). "Being 'Good' Isn't the Only Way to Go," *Houston Chronicle*, p. B2.

viii. K. Mishra, L. Boynton, A. Mishra (2014). "Driving Employee Engagement: the Expanded Role of Internal Communications," *International Journal of Business Communication* 51, no. 2, p. 191.

ix. A. Bryant.

x. D. McGregor (1960). *The Human Side of Enterprise* (New York, NY: McGraw-Hill).

xi. Edelman (2012). "Edelman Trust Barometer: Executive Summary," Retrieved from http://www.scribd.com/doc/79026497/2012-Edelman-Trust-Barometer-Executive-Summary

xii. G. Hammill (2005). "Mixing and Managing Four Generations of Employees," *FDR Magazine Online*, Retrieved from http://www.fdu.edu/newspubs/magazine/05ws/generations.htm

PART 3

Get it Done

CHAPTER 6

Strategies for Communicating Job Expectations

So far in this book we've looked at strategies that will help you "get along" at work. We've described communication techniques you can use to find out what's going on around you and strengthen your work relationships. Networking is an invaluable survival skill in today's diverse workplace, and building an open, trusting environment allows employees to perform at their peak.

After you've learned how to get along with everyone on the job, you need to find ways to "get it done," which is the theme of this section. It's all about the daily workplace interaction skills that you as a manager need in order to keep your people motivated and productive. Wouldn't your job be simple if people did what they were supposed to do and thought that their paychecks were sufficient reward? But a manager's work isn't simple, because every day you are dealing with human nature.

This section on how to "get it done" includes four chapters. Chapter 6 gives you strategies for making sure your employees understand what they are supposed to do on the job. Chapter 7 explains how to respond when subordinates don't do what they are supposed to do and how to give corrective feedback. Continuing our examination of tough communication challenges that you face every day, Chapter 8 discusses conflict and offers five strategies for managing it. Chapter 9 focuses on another communication challenge—figuring out when someone is being dishonest with you.

Communicating Job Expectations

If you've ever been surprised and disappointed when a subordinate said, "I don't know how to do that" or "I didn't know you wanted me to do that," this chapter is for you. Just because a new hire supposedly has the job qualifications a position requires, that doesn't guarantee that he can hit the ground running. Rather than assuming he will step right in, it's important to take the time to communicate your expectations as clearly and completely as you can. That will not only reduce the employee's performance anxiety, it will also build a trusting relationship. Additionally, it will minimize the frequency of the corrective actions described in Chapter 7.

The Tell-Show-Do Formula

The classic model for teaching new employees how to do a job is "tell-show-do." I stumbled on this model when I was an 18-year-old college freshman. I had been working part-time as a file clerk at the Credit Bureau of Cook County for the previous 2 years. When my supervisor heard that I had recently graduated from high school and was now in college, she decided that my new educational status qualified me to become the trainer on the night shift. Figure 6.1 shows the training model I followed.

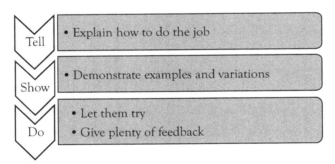

Figure 6.1 Training Model

Back then, credit records consisted of envelopes with pieces of paper in them that detailed car loan terms, department store credit card activity, home mortgages, liens, collections, and the like. The envelopes were filed in enormous metal cabinets in an enormous building in downtown Chicago. Yes, it's true—this was during the pretechnology era. For security reasons, a fairly sophisticated coding system was used for organizing the files rather than alphabetical order. My assignment was to train the newly hired nightshift clerks on the coding system so they could find files and report the information in them to our clients.

Tell

I first found some codebooks, made copies, and laminated them. I called them cheat sheets, though I later learned the term, "job aids." Each class began with me going through the cheat sheets with the trainees, telling them how to decode existing file contents and how to code new information. I quizzed them on the codes as we went along, to hasten their memorization. I told them about the rules, procedures, and policies that governed the work they would be expected to do.

Show

Next I wheeled a basket of credit files into the training room, picked one file out of the basket at random, opened it, showed the trainees what was inside, and helped them to understand what each number and piece of paper meant. They watched as I handled the material, filing and refiling it properly, explaining variations. The basic idea behind this step was to demonstrate examples of the work they would be expected to perform, and "non-examples" of mistakes to avoid.

Do

During our last class, I gave each trainee a basket of files and let them go through it themselves, figuring out what it contained and why the information was organized the way it was. They worked in teams while I stood by, guiding, encouraging, and answering questions that their teammates couldn't. On "graduation night", the trainees returned to the main floor, and I shadowed them as they applied their new skills in the actual work environment, coaching them along and handling problems.

You may be interested to know that my little tell-show-do method at the Credit Bureau was pioneered by an American educational psychologist named Robert Gagne, who had worked with the Army Air Corps during World War II to train pilots. After the war, he spent the rest of his career perfecting and testing his instructional design model, first publishing it in 1965 as the "Nine Events of Instruction."[i] Since then, extensive research has validated Gagne's principles in educational settings, though I know from first-hand experience that the principles also apply to work settings.[ii]

Formal Training Programs

If you want your employees to do certain tasks and they aren't doing them correctly, don't jump to conclusions about their motivations, work attitudes, or intellect. First, check to be sure that they understand what you expect them to do. The following paragraphs will provide an overview of the training cycle, taking you through the process of determining what employees know and don't know, designing and delivering formal training programs, and conducting follow-up evaluations.

Training Cycle:

1. Conduct a needs assessment
2. Design instructional materials
3. Determine logistics
4. Help adults learn
5. Evaluate outcomes

1. **Conduct a needs assessment.** The most obvious way to determine what employees already know and don't know is to ask. But if you say, "Do you know how to do this?" they will usually say, "Yes, I do" out of fear that they will look incompetent.

   Instead, try an open-ended question such as, "Tell me (or show me) how you do this." The gap between what they are doing and what you want them to do is the need for training. The goal of training is to close that gap between actual and optimal behaviors.

Optimal behavior − Actual behavior = Training Need

   I will pause here to say that the training needs assessment (TNA) process not only determines important deviations from a standard. Managers can also use the TNA process to anticipate changes in standards and prepare employees to meet them. Thus, needs assessment can be proactive as well as reactive. Similarly, employees' learning needs can be considered as an opportunity as well as a problem. In short, training facilitates change. An instrument I have used in my consulting practice for determining communication training needs can be found in Appendix 1.

Of course, you can't solve every performance problem through training. Environmental barriers, employee conflicts, equipment and supply issues, and cultural differences are just a few factors that you must consider when analyzing reasons for poor employee performance. But if your gap analysis shows that the employees need training, the second step is to design an instructional program.

2. **Design instructional materials.** Remember my story about training at the Credit Bureau of Cook County? Putting yourself in the shoes of the new hires, which do you think was more effective—reading the codebooks, listening to my explanations, or watching my demonstrations?

Extensive research shows that most people are visual learners. That is, they remember what they see better than what they read or hear. In fact, listening is one of the poorest ways to learn for most people.

As Figure 6.2 shows, if your employees just listen, they will lose 90 percent of what you say after 3 days.[iii] For maximum retention, you need to appeal to a combination of senses—give them something to look at, something to listen to, and something to read.

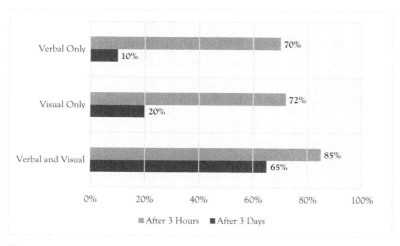

Figure 6.2 Percent of Audience Recall

I'm embarrassed to tell you this story, but it's true. One day, at a former employer organization, new, sophisticated phones suddenly appeared in our offices. We all dutifully went to training and watched demonstrations of the various snazzy features of the phones. We were given laminated cards to take along; I put mine right under the phone on my desk. Later, when I had to do something tricky, like forwarding a call or putting a call on hold while I picked up another line, I fumbled. I stuck my head out the office door and yelled, "Will someone help me forward a call?" The transfer of learning had failed.

Why? Yes, you guessed it; none of us in the phone training program had been given a chance to try using the new system under the trainer's eye. They had skipped the "Do" in the tell-show-do model.

In summary, instructional materials should appeal to a range of senses—sight, touch, sound, even taste—and involve a range of activities. Dreary lectures don't work well. The rule of training is, change things up every 20 minutes.

3. **Determine logistics**. Once you have determined the need for training and put together some materials, you must figure out when, where, and how the training will be delivered. If employees are called off the job site so they can attend training, who will take their place, allowing the workflow to continue? What about the costs? Logistical issues can be daunting, so let's take them one at a time.

    Many organizations have turned to computer-assisted delivery (CAD) in order to avoid logistical barriers. CAD programs are popular because they can be efficient and cost effective. Typically, employees sit at a computer and work through the training package at their own pace, and sometimes on their own time. Built-in measures of progress along the way can ensure that they don't just click through the material. Evidence of completion and test scores can be automatically reported back to the work unit and to human resources.

    Face-to-face training classes, by comparison, are more time consuming and often more costly because of trainees' time away from work. Sessions are intensive but often more effective in terms of actual learning and facilitating behavior changes. Outside trainers can provide a fresh, unbiased viewpoint and a threat-free resource.

In my years as an external consultant and trainer, many times trainees have approached me during breaks, wanting to speak privately about troubling situations on the job. They have confided self-doubts, frustrations, and a need for information that they were unwilling to bring up to their supervisors. And believe it or not, sometimes their supervisors were even identified as the cause of their problems. As a communication specialist, I readily provide extra resources and information to the trainees, but I avoid ethical dilemmas by reminding them who is paying me, and that I must report to management any issues that come up. Then I tactfully suggest ways they can approach their superiors with the issue.

After deciding on the delivery format—CAD or face-to-face—you will have to select a training source. Often, your human resources office will help you find a vendor, either internal or external. Customized training is usually more costly than "off the shelf" prepackaged programs, but in the end it can be more effective because it is aimed at a narrower target of training needs.

You may have to get creative in finding ways to cut costs. Here's one example. Once a consulting client, a small manufacturing company, scheduled my training program between 4:00 and 7:00 pm in the company's training room. Trainees were on the clock until 5:00, meaning that the company paid them for that first hour of training. Between 5:00 and 6:00 everyone enjoyed a potluck dinner (a kitchen was adjacent to the training room). Then from 6:00 until 7:00 we continued the training on the employees' own time.

Another logistical issue is who should attend. One consulting client made it mandatory for everyone from the receptionist to the president to come to communication training. At the same time. In one big room. You can imagine the uncomfortable silences when I brought up certain topics.

Another client, a law firm, hired me to conduct a teambuilding workshop with the firm's office assistants in an attempt to improve communication between the attorneys and their admins. When I suggested that the attorneys would benefit from attending the sessions, too, they balked. To convince the attorneys, I compared it to marriage counseling with just one spouse. Interestingly, the attorneys who did find time to show up had the fewest communication break-downs with their staff.

4. **Help adults learn**. Logistical issues are complex. Often you have to make do with an imperfect schedule, compromising on time, place, and length. But once you've nailed down those decisions, you can move on to considering how adults learn best.

A typical face-to-face training class should be organized like this:

Organization of Face-to-face Training Session

Beginning
- Set goals
- Describe appropriate behaviors
- Explain methods
- Motivate participants to learn

Middle
- Broadcast structure of the program
- Balance lecture, discussion, practice, Q & A sessions
- Make learning fun, not frightening

End
- Review achievements
- Discuss transfer of learning to the work environment
- Suggest ways to reinforce the learning and overcome roadblocks
- Give rewards

Notice the level of trainee involvement in each segment. Adults learn best when they see the value of the learning. So in order to buy into the training, they must be able to connect the information with their own goals. They should be actively engaged every step of the way.

Research on how adults learn indicates that there are four learning styles, as identified in Figure 6.3: personal, analytical, practical, and innovative.[iv] Becoming aware of the diversity of learning styles will make you a more culturally competent manager.

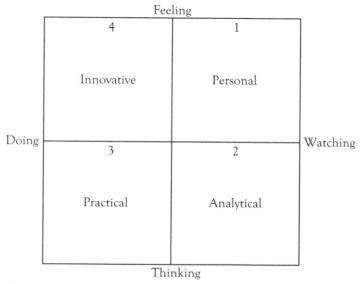

Figure 6.3 Learning Styles

In the next paragraphs, we will examine the four adult learning styles and consider training techniques to suit each.

The *Personal Learner* is high on feeling and watching. This style will relate material to their personal experience and do well discussing in groups, sharing their feelings, and interacting.

The *Analytical Learner* is high on thinking and watching. This style needs to know how facts relate to established knowledge and will do well in highly structured, systematic learning environments, lectures, and case studies.

The *Practical Learner* is high on doing and thinking. This style is results oriented and will do well in hands-on activities and simulations.

The *Innovative Learner* is high on doing and feeling. This style resists structure, enjoys considering possibilities, and flourishes when free to brainstorm and experiment.

Taking the time to identify your employees' preferred learning styles and developing training materials to suit them will pay off.

Realize, however, that while it's not always practical or even possible, the best solution is to find a balance between nurturing and challenging (Figure 6.4). That is, try to build some elements into the training program that will maximize each learning style. For example, you could incorporate a group discussion for the personal learners, a brainstorming activity for the innovative learners, a case study for the analytical learners, and a simulation for the practical learners.

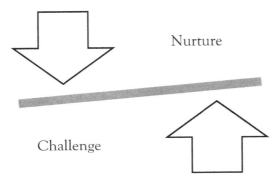

Nurture

Challenge

Figure 6.4 Balancing Act for Facilitating Learning

A training program that attempts to close the gap between actual and optimal behaviors, that is delivered in an efficient yet effective format, and that incorporates techniques designed to facilitate every learning style is likely to be successful. The final step is to evaluate.

5. **Evaluate outcomes.** After your employees have received training, how can you be sure that it will stick? Donald Kirkpatrick, a top researcher in corporate training and development, identified four levels of evaluation and suggested that there are numerous ways to determine success.[v]

The first level of evaluation is the trainees' *reaction*. Immediately post-program, ask the trainees how they liked the training. Usually you can accomplish this with a satisfaction survey that asks for ratings of the instructor, the materials, the logistics, and the topics. Such a survey is generally referred to as a "smile sheet." Typically, comments are limited to sweeping statements like, "the instructor was very lively," "I learned a lot," and "The room was too cold."

The second level of evaluation is trainee *learning*. Usually you can accomplish this with a test that you administer immediately post-program or after a short time has passed. Scores will indicate how much the trainees actually learned and remembered.

The third level of evaluation is trainee *behavior*. This is often the most important to managers, because it measures whether the trainees can apply the new information back on the job. If this "transfer of training" does not occur, however, look for barriers other than trainee's ability. You may identify attitudinal and even environmental barriers to changing their behaviors.

The fourth level of evaluation is *results*. You can usually leave this level of evaluation to human resources, finance, and operations executives who have access to data about your work unit's productivity and performance pre- and post-training. Identifying the elements that affect return on investment (ROI) can be slippery, since many factors other than employee competence will influence company performance.

Kirkpatrick's Levels of Training Evaluation:

1. Reaction
2. Learning
3. Behavior
4. Results

Let's examine a case to see how the levels of training evaluation can work.

The Case of the Unused Equipment

Memorial Hospitals Group purchases new intravenous feeding equipment because it is more comfortable, safer, cleaner, and precisely controllable. Approximately one-third of the total units are in place in the hospitals, but few of them are being used. The new equipment comes with information on how to maintain and use it. Still, staff avoids the new and relies on the old. Prior to purchasing thousands of additional IV units, management wants to make sure that the new ones are as good as promised. They can't check them out or provide better service to patients if the staff avoids the new equipment.

What Causes the Gap between Optimal and Actual Behaviors at Memorial Hospitals Group?

Possible Cause	Questions to Ask
Skill/Knowledge	Does the IV work?
	Does staff know how to set up and maintain the IV?
	Is it a tougher process than the former IV?
Incentive	What happens if they use it? If they don't?
	How do supervisors respond to it?
Environment	Is the IV there? Where it's supposed to be?
	Is the old IV equally accessible?
Motivation	Does the staff know why the IV has appeared?
	Does the staff believe they can master the new IV?

This case demonstrates that employee knowledge and skills may be just one of many factors affecting workplace behavior. Furthermore, training aimed at closing the perceived gap between optimal and actual behavior might fail simply because training was not the cause of the problem in the first place. Solid evaluation methods will reveal reasons for training success and failure.

Summary

This chapter has provided guidelines for communicating performance expectations to your employees. To determine whether subordinates understand what you want them to do, you ask the right questions. If the conclusion is "no," the next step is to help them learn the expected tasks. You can explain by following the "tell-show-do" approach. When more formal instruction is called for, you can design, develop, and deliver a training program. You can help assure successful performance outcomes by effectively applying the five steps in the training process: assessing needs, developing instructional materials, making logistical arrangements, facilitating adult learning styles, and evaluating outcomes.

Endnotes

i. R. Gagne. "Nine Events of Instruction," Retrieved from http://www. instructionaldesign.org/theories/conditions-learning.html

ii. J.L. Garner (2011). "How Award-Winning Professors in Higher Education Use Merrill's First Principles of Instruction," *International Journal of Instructional Technology and Distance Learning* 8, no, 5, pp. 3–16. See also: M.D. Merrill (2002). "First Principles of Instruction," *Educational Technology Research and Development* 50, no. 3, pp. 43–59.

iii. C. Hamilton (2013). *Communicating for Results: A Guide for Business and the Professions*, 10th ed. (Cengage).

iv. D. Kolb, R. Fry (1975). "Toward an Applied Theory of Experiential Learning", in *Theories of Group Process,* ed. C. Cooper (London: John Wiley). See also http://learningfromexperience.com

v. D. Kirkpatrick, J.D. Kirkpatrick (2007). *Implementing the Four Levels* (Oakland, CA: Berrett-Koehler Publishers).

CHAPTER 7

Strategies for Giving Corrective Feedback

In the previous chapter, we considered strategies for explaining your performance expectations to subordinates. After communicating job responsibilities, managers need to give feedback to employees about how well they are doing the job. This chapter offers strategies for correcting inappropriate workplace behavior and for maximizing the value of formal performance review interviews. It concludes by showing you how to develop an open communication climate that will support continued performance improvement.

Handling Inappropriate Behavior

Whenever you notice an employee performing inappropriately, you should immediately deal with it. Don't store it and wait until formal performance review time to bring it up. The time-honored formula for correcting subordinates' inappropriate behavior is DESC, which you probably learned during a supervisory training class. DESC works because it is based on the principles of behavioral psychology. Briefly, it goes like this.

> D = Describe
> E = Express
> S = Specify
> C = Consequences

1. **Describe** the inappropriate behavior. It's important that you focus on behavior, or actions, rather than attitudes. For example, if you are

dealing with a chronically tardy subordinate, you should describe the behavior concretely: "John, you've shown up at least 10 minutes late for your shift four times in the past 2 weeks." This sentence sticks to the facts.

Don't confuse observations of behavior with assumptions about what's behind them. An observation or fact is something you can check. It is either true or false. An assumption is an opinion. It is neither true nor false, it's just an opinion. If you start talking to your subordinate about attitudes, such as, "John, you're lazy and unreliable," you are going to have trouble defending your claims. John is going to deny, deflect, and defend himself by responding with something like, "That's just your opinion." And he'll be right. That conversation is doomed.

2. **Express** why the behavior is inappropriate. This step is critical because you have to come up with a good reason for requiring a change in the behavior. If you can't justify the change, your employee is unlikely to put in the effort. Sometimes managers will stoop to excuses like, "It's the policy" in an attempt to justify a required change, despite knowing how weak that sounds. Aren't you reminded of all the times your parents tried to correct your behavior when you were a child and justified their demands with, "Because I said so"? You didn't accept it then, and your subordinate certainly won't accept it now.

   The following story will demonstrate the importance of step 2. Once a client organization asked me to coach a manager on his communication skills. In preparation, I talked with some of his subordinates. Among their complaints was that every morning he set an alarm clock to go off loudly at 8:00 a.m. in the office. When I asked the manager why he did that, he said it was his way of reminding the employees of the importance of promptness. They thought it was demeaning. So I asked the manager why promptness was so important, other than that it was the rule. After thinking about it for a while, he came up with a good explanation that had to do with being ready to pick up the phones when the customers started calling and placing orders. Once the manager expressed this valid reason that tardiness was inappropriate, the office workers' behaviors improved.

3. **Specify** the behavior you want the employee to adopt. Again, the emphasis here is on behaviors rather than attitudes. You must tell your employees exactly what you want them to do. That should include how often, beginning when, and with what degree of accuracy.

   An example of a specific behavior to be adopted goes like this: "Beginning Monday morning, every time someone calls, please pick up the phone before the third ring and say, "Baxter and Thompson Law Offices. Mona speaking. How may I help you?" You can see that this instruction is better than something vague like, "Answer the phone quickly and professionally."

4. Tell the **consequences** of adopting and not adopting the behavior. This step may seem obvious. Most companies have disciplinary procedures in place that human resources will gladly explain to you. The procedures may include something like, "the first warning is oral, the second is written, the third is punished by an hour's pay deduction, the fourth is a week's suspension, and the fifth is dismissal." Employees should be well aware of the penalties for offenses. Policy and procedure manuals are supposed to include clear consequences for employee violations of the policies and procedures.

   You may wonder why subordinates sometimes persist in doing what they know they shouldn't, such as coming in late or using office technology for personal reasons. Behavioral psychologists have shown that behavior is shaped by a pattern of rewards. But what could possibly be a worker's reward for ignoring policy and coming to work late? Well, less time spent working, for one thing—that's a major reward for many people! And if there are no negative consequences that counteract the reward, such as docked pay, the worker will be motivated to do it again. Other possible rewards for inappropriate behaviors include getting attention from the boss and/or coworkers, retribution for perceived slights, and an enhanced self-image for defying authority. Simply put, if you want a behavior to stop, figure out the reward and withhold it.

   But what about the other part of step 4—telling the consequences for correcting a behavior? "Oh, that's easy," you may say. "If the employees adopt the behaviors I expect, they get to keep their jobs." True, but is that enough motivation to make them change?

Often it isn't. What usually happens is that employees try the new behavior in a goodwill effort, but as soon as they hit a bump in the road, they revert to their old behavior, despite knowing that it's inappropriate, because of the lack of reward. It's easier to backslide than to keep trying to make the change.

- Reward subordinates when they do something right.
- Don't reward them when they do something wrong.

Are there any other rewards you can offer for compliance besides job security? You might think the only reward available is a raise in pay. But you shouldn't have to give people a raise just for doing their work correctly, which is the minimum standard for employment. Creative, skilled, respected managers know that workers are motivated by more than money; they have deep-seated needs for attention, recognition, affiliation, and approval. Therefore, saying "Thank you for your contributions," and, "I noticed how hard you worked on that project," and, " You did a good job getting that account" will often be enough reward and reinforcement for maintenance of the new behavior. You may have noticed that such non-monetary reinforcement works especially well with your best employees.

As you read in Chapter 4, positive interpersonal relationships between managers and their subordinates are powerful motivators. Can you say "thanks" too often? Probably not. The words don't lose their power to make people feel valued. After many years of marriage, I still appreciate hearing my spouse say, "Thank you for a good meal" when I cook dinner. So does he. Simply put, if you want a behavior to start or continue, figure out a meaningful reward and provide it.

Performance Reviews

Periodically, you are called on to conduct formal performance reviews of your subordinates. Almost 60 years ago, Maier cited several purposes for the performance review[i] and current objectives remain much the same.

- Let employees know where they stand.
- Recognize good work.
- Communicate to subordinates how they should improve.
- Develop employees in their present jobs.
- Develop and train employees for higher jobs.
- Assess the department or unit as a whole and where each person fits into the larger picture.

While the benefits of formal performance reviews seem obvious, in fact many managers conduct them ineffectively and reluctantly. Samuel Culbert, a professor of management at the University of California—Los Angeles, and author of *Get Rid of the Performance Review!*, calls it "the most ridiculous practice in the world [because] it's ... fraudulent, dishonest at its core, and reflects ... cowardly management." Culbert sees performance reviews as a way to intimidate employees and concludes that they do more harm than good.[ii]

This contradiction exists for several reasons, including that managers do not like to be put into the role of evaluator. Some managers may fear that the discomfort created by a poorly conducted performance review will destroy their working relationship with subordinates. Another reason may be that managers haven't been adequately trained to conduct these interviews.[iii] If you hesitate to provide corrective feedback because you fear you might drive your valuable employee to the competition, the following information will help your performance reviews have better outcomes.

Preparation Steps for Performance Reviews:

1. Purpose
2. Timing
3. Location
4. Content
5. Outcome

Purpose

Typically, performance reviews (1) focus on the worker's past performance or (2) focus on the worker's future performance, including goal setting that leads to improvement. The ideal review will cover both purposes, plus two more: (3) focus on the supervisor's past performance and (4) focus on the supervisor's future performance, including goal setting that leads to being a better boss. Thus, a formal opportunity for two-way feedback about the past and the future will benefit both parties. Remember, though, that there should be no surprises in a performance review. If you've dealt with negative behaviors on the spot and rewarded positive behaviors as you caught them, and if your relationship with your subordinate is open and honest, then both of you will already know what to expect during a formal evaluation session.

Timing

Formal reviews are most often conducted at least once a year, with the understanding that the manager's feedback should be given to employees whenever needed. There should be no surprises during a formal review because it should be a summary of all the prior conversations between managers and their subordinates about positive feedback, corrective feedback, career path, and compensation.

Why perform a formal review once a year when you provide regular, frequent feedback? Periodic "course correction" makes sense for even very satisfactory subordinates. Also, certain situations, such as the completion of a major project or unusually poor performance, require formal feedback. Consider the entire situation when determining the best time for a performance interview.

Once you've selected the time, tell the employees well in advance so they can prepare psychologically. Avoid the "stop by my office as soon as you get a chance" type of announcement.

Location

Once the purpose and timing are set, consider the best place for the interview. Managers tend to schedule the performance review in their own offices without realizing how potentially threatening this environment may be, especially when the subordinate is not accustomed to spending much time in the manager's office. Often, the best place for the interview is a neutral, safe, private location that maximizes two-way interaction.

Message Content

Next, focus on the content of the session. Regardless of the specific purpose, review the dimensions of the subordinate's job, review notes from the previous performance review and recent job occurrences. You may even want to ask customers, peers, or other managers for their feedback about the employee. Appendix 2 of this book includes an example of a tool for gathering concrete feedback from other employees about the person being evaluated. After gathering all your feedback documents, list specific items you want to cover in the performance review interview.

During the interview, the more you let your subordinate talk, the more likely that open and valuable communication will result. Studies show that managers who encourage a self-review of performance are more satisfying than those based strictly on manager-prepared appraisals.[iv] For useful feedback in both directions and reasonable goal setting, you must establish trust through two-way communication.

If you have lots of negative feedback to convey, you might be tempted to use the old "sandwich" format; however, I don't recommend it. In the sandwich approach, you place a negative statement between two positive ones. Most employees quickly recognize this as manipulative and they discount the praise. A better procedure is to begin the performance review with positive feedback and ask the employee open questions such as, "What accomplishments are you most proud of this year?" This tactic helps to establish a supportive climate and two-way interaction. Once aware that you do appreciate past success, the subordinate becomes more receptive to corrective feedback.[v]

Outcome

At the end of the performance review, be sure that you and your subordinate compose action plans for improvement. Both of you should contribute to each other's action plans, and both of you should agree on them. They should be behavior-based, specific, concrete, achievable, and challenging. To show seriousness of intent, you might each sign them. These action plans may be in addition to the employee appraisal forms that your human resources department expects you to complete. The key is to create a perception of a common goal that you both will work toward. A template for a work plan that I use in my consulting practice is in Appendix 3 at the back of this book.

Action plan contents:

- What I will do
- When I will do it
- With whom I will do it
- What I expect to be the result
- How I will know I am successful

Performance Feedback for Culturally Diverse Workers

Formal performance appraisals are unique to U.S. work environments. In most other countries, especially collectivist and high power difference cultures, the assumption is that workers will always give 100 percent (Chapter 2). This attitude may be grounded in the fact that a single family often controls an entire industry, so if you want to work in a particular business, you had better be born into that family or try to marry into it. When you work for family, you continually give your best effort to make the business profitable and the family prosperous. Deep involvement and commitment make feedback from managers unnecessary.

A more complex situation occurs when workers in a U.S. business come from one of these other cultures. For example, in a manufacturing company that was one of my clients, the laborers were predominantly Vietnamese, while the production managers and supervisors were Anglo-American and Hispanic. The managers had difficulty getting their workers to take direction; they typically ignored both positive and negative feedback. Close observation revealed that the workers listened only to their Vietnamese elders on the shop floor. From then on, the managers simply told the elders what they wanted from the workers, and the elders made sure it happened.

Defensive and Supportive Communication Climates

In order to establish a trusting environment during the performance review and even during informal feedback sessions, you need to create and maintain a supportive communication climate. Table 7.1 draws on Jack Gibbs' classic work that shows you what to say and how to say it.[vi]

Table 7.1 Defensive and Supportive Climates

Defensive Climate	Supportive Climate
Evaluative	Descriptive
Control	Problem orientation
Neutrality	Empathy
Superiority	Equality
Certainty	Provisionalism

In the following discussion, you will see concrete examples of statements that contrast the two climates.

Evaluative versus Descriptive

Communication that blames a subordinate naturally leads to a defensive climate. Avoid statements that make moral judgments or that question their values and motives. Descriptive communication provides specific feedback, not opinions.

Evaluative	Descriptive
You simply have to stop making so many silly mistakes.	We're still getting more than three errors per run with the new system.
Betty, you're tactless and rude.	Betty, some people say your humor is offensive.
The delay was definitely your fault because you didn't follow instructions.	There seems to be some confusion about the instructions.

Control versus Problem Orientation

Problem-oriented communication defines a mutual problem and seeks a solution. Controlling communication tries to do "something" to another person such as forcing a change in a behavior or an attitude. The problem orientation conveys respect for the employee's ability to work on a problem and to find answers to the problem.

Control	Problem Orientation
Here is what you can do to reduce errors.	What do you think we can do to reduce errors?
You definitely have a problem with that project.	We've got a problem with this project.
Stop being so negative around here.	How do you think we could develop a more positive approach?

As you can see, the problem-oriented comments develop more opportunities for two-way communication by using open-ended questions. Listening is also a productive by-product of the problem orientation.

Neutrality versus Empathy

Neutrality expresses a lack of concern for the well-being of the employee, while empathy shows that you identify with the subordinate's problem, share her feelings, and accept the emotional values involved.

Neutrality	Empathy
That really isn't much of a problem.	Sounds like you're really concerned about it. Tell me more about the situation.
Everybody has to face that at one time or another.	That can be a tough situation. I'll tell you how I've seen it handled before, and then you can give me your reaction.
Well, everyone is entitled to an opinion.	I think we disagree. Let's discuss this further and compare viewpoints.

You show empathy in the performance review when you ask how the employee feels about something, and when you attempt to understand and accept the employee's feelings.

Superiority versus Equality

The less the psychological distance between you and the subordinate, the greater the probability of an effective performance review. Managers often stifle subordinates by subtly indicating both verbally and nonverbally their superior position, wealth, power, intelligence, or even physical characteristics. Sitting behind a big desk, putting your feet on the desk, looking uninterested, and acting busy are all signs of superiority. Showing superiority can only add to defensiveness and reduce two-way communication.

Superiority	Equality
After working on this kind of problem for 10 years, I know how to handle it.	This solution has worked before, so it should work here too.
I'm paid more than you, so it is my responsibility to make this decision.	It's my ultimate responsibility to make the decision, but I sure want your recommendations.
The type of problems I face shouldn't be of interest to people at your level.	I want to share with you the type of situations I'm involved with.

Instead of telling the subordinate what to do, ask permission. Instead of saying, "Rewrite this report and correct all the mistakes," try, "May I make a suggestion? I can show you an easy way to find your mistakes and correct them." This approach removes the barrier of "Don't tell me what to do!"

Certainty versus Provisionalism

Managers who emphasize certainty often phrase what they say as if the decision can't be changed. This dogmatic approach makes the employee feel that offering new ideas or a different solution is a waste of time. Provisionalism demonstrates that you are willing to be challenged to arrive at the best possible solution. Provisionalism promotes enthusiasm and provides a challenge to employees.

Certainty	Provisionalism
I know what the problem is, so there isn't much reason to talk about it.	I have some ideas, but it would be good to talk about it.
This is the way it's going to be done.	Let's try it this way for a while and see what happens.
I want it to be completed by June 1.	What needs to be done to ensure that it's completed by June 1?

These five elements of an effective communication strategy—description, problem orientation, empathy, equality, and provisionalism—are major factors in reducing defensiveness and developing trust. Once trust has developed, your feedback to subordinates is more often accepted and taken seriously.

Summary

"Getting it done" calls for knowing strategies for corrective feedback, so you can motivate your employees to higher levels of performance. Your subordinates will see feedback as constructive rather than as negative criticism if you keep in mind the following principles:

1. Describe the inappropriate behavior. Avoid criticism and claims about motives, intents, and feelings.
2. Explain why it's inappropriate.
3. Focus feedback on a limited number of observable behaviors that you want the subordinate to adopt.
4. Tell the subordinate what will happen if she or he adopts the new behavior and what will happen if she or he doesn't.

To ensure that the objectives or action plans are clear, write them down. Action plans guide employees' future activities to achieve established goals.

As a manager, you are responsible for the performance appraisal process. The challenge is to balance the needs of the organization with the needs of your subordinates. If you approach performance reviews fairly and without bias, you can achieve your objectives and grow your own managerial skills in the process.

Your subordinates are more likely to accept corrective feedback when you have created a supportive communication climate. By using a communication strategy that is descriptive, problem-oriented, empathic, equal, and provisional, you will reduce defensiveness and develop trust.

Endnotes

i. R.F. Maier (1958). *The Appraisal Interview: Objectives and Skills* (New York, NY: John Wiley & Sons), p. 3.

ii. S.A. Culbert (2010). *Get Rid of the Performance Review! How Companies Can Stop Intimidating, Start Managing, and Focus on What Really Matters* (New York, NY: Hachette Book Group).

iii. B. Dugan (1988). "Effects of Assessor Training on Information Use," *Journal of Applied Psychology* 73, pp. 743–48; and T.M. Downs (1990). "Predictions of Communication Satisfaction during Performance Appraisal Interviews," *Management Communication Quarterly* 3, no. 13, pp. 334–54.

iv. B.E. Becker, R.J. Klimoski (1989). "A Field Study of the Relationship Between the Organizational Feedback Environment and Performance," *Personnel Psychology* 42, no. 3, pp. 343–58.

v. D. Cederblom (1992). "The Performance Appraisal Interview: A Review, Implications, and Suggestions," in *Readings in Organizational Communication,* ed. K.L. Hutchinson (Dubuque, IA: Wm. C. Brown), pp. 310–21.

vi. J.R. Gibb (1961). "Defensive Communication," *Journal of Communication,* 11, no. 3, pp. 141–48.

CHAPTER 8

Strategies for Managing Conflict

"Getting it done" is all about daily workplace interactions. So far in Part Three we've talked about how to communicate your job expectations to your subordinates (Chapter 6) and how to give subordinates corrective feedback (Chapter 7). Continuing our examination of tough communication challenges that you face every day, this chapter looks at conflict. Included are strategies for managing clashes between you and your boss, you and your coworkers, and you and your subordinates.

We'll first distinguish between destructive and constructive conflict; you may be surprised to learn that conflict can benefit you and your company. Then we'll peek behind the curtain to learn why conflict is always such a strong presence, especially in diverse workplaces. Finally, and probably most important to you, we'll show you five strategies for dealing with conflict and explain when each one works best.

Tensions can run high at work. As a manager, you are likely to spend up to 35 percent of your time dealing with complaints and handling disruptions in your fast-paced, diverse work environment.[i] Conflict may range from a simple disagreement over a work procedure to an argument over priorities, to a work stoppage, and even to violence. The incidence of workplace violence continues to increase at an alarming rate. Violence is the number one cause of death on the job for women, and the number two cause for men. It's a manager's duty to protect workers from violence by developing intervention efforts.

When is conflict beneficial and when is it harmful? What causes conflict, anyway? What methods can you use to resolve conflict? Is any single method best? The following discussion answers these questions.

Pros and Cons of Workplace Conflict

Conflict generally is considered a negative influence that is destructive; however, it can be a positive influence if you manage it properly. Conflict forces you to analyze goals, it creates dialogue among employees, and it fosters creative solutions. It has been linked to organizational learning, and even to improved performance and productivity. Without conflict, employees and organizations would stagnate.

Conflict between diverse age groups is one example of how conflict can be positive. For the first time in U.S. history, four generations are working together. Conflict commonly is due to differences in their work style and philosophy. Older workers view "work" as a place—a location you go to at a specified time, such as 9 a.m. to 5 p.m. Younger workers tend to view "work" as something you do—anywhere, any time. They grew up in a digital world where information is always available. So it's easy for Boomers to conclude that Millennials who arrive at 9:30 a.m. are working less hard than they, who arrived at 8:30 a.m., not realizing that the younger generation may have already put in time at their home computers or smartphones while still in pajamas. To Millennials, rigid scheduling of work is unnecessary. Boomers can benefit from their younger coworkers by learning that much of today's work can be done in flextime for maximum efficiency.

Conflict may also foster creativity. It helps to overcome biases by forcing you out of your traditional ways of thinking. In this way, conflict promotes the unstructured thinking that lets you develop good, novel alternatives to difficult problems.[ii]

In addition, decisions are better when there is open opposition and resistance. In one study, high-quality decisions occurred in 46 percent of the situations with strong worker resistance, but in only 19 percent of the situations where resistance was weak or nonexistent.[iii]

Thus, if you are a manager who prides yourself on running a smooth ship, you may not be as effective as you think. The smooth ship may reflect suppressed conflict that could have potential benefit if allowed free play. In fact, the conflict might not be as harmful as suppressing it is.

Benefits of Conflict:

- Forces goal analysis
- Creates dialogue among employees
- Fosters creative solutions
- Stimulates organizational learning
- Improves performance and productivity
- Prevents stagnation

Causes of Workplace Conflict

When you perceive conflict in the workplace, you may assume it's due to incompatible personalities. "Why can't everyone just get along?" you plead. But once you understand that the sources of conflict are often deeper than individual personality, then you will be able to select the right communication strategy for handling it.

The underlying causes of conflict are often the organization's hierarchy, ways of doing business, and a built-in opposition between units. Research shows that conflict increases with levels of hierarchy, standardization of jobs, and the number of workers.

The distribution of the limited resources available in an organization is another source of conflict. If resources were unlimited, few conflicts would arise, but this condition seldom exists. When resources are limited, and more than one person or group wants a share, conflict and competition develop.

Diverse goals are another source of organizational conflict. For instance, clashes may occur between Quality Assurance and Production in a manufacturing company. The goal of the quality control people is zero defects, while the goal of the production unit is filling the customers' orders on time. Conflicting goals and roles can also explain why a company's sales people routinely ignore the accounting staff's requests for expense receipts. Or why a shift foreman refuses to let his workers attend an employee development session offered by human resources. To reduce such traditional conflicts between functional units, managers should remind their people of the overarching goals, mission, and vision.

Sources of Conflict:

- The organization's hierarchy
- Ways of doing business
- Built-in opposition between units
- Highly standardized jobs
- Large number of workers
- Distribution of limited resources
- Diverse goals

Strategies for Managing Conflict

Once you have pinpointed the sources of workplace conflict, you are ready to manage the conflict. This section offers strategies for managing conflict up the ladder of power and authority, across the ladder with peers, and down the ladder with subordinates. While reviewing these strategies, keep in mind that different conflict situations call for different strategies, so effective communication means that you match the strategy to the situation.

Managing Conflict with the Boss: Avoid

You might think that the best way to handle conflict with your boss is to avoid it. The avoidance or withdrawal strategy combines a low concern for production with a low concern for people. If you use this style a lot, you see conflict as useless. Rather than undergo the tension and frustration of conflict, you use avoidance simply to remove yourself from conflict situations, either physically or psychologically. You dislike tension, don't take sides in a disagreement among others, and feel little commitment to any decisions reached. This conflict management style is the second most popular among U.S. managers.

Avoidance doesn't need to be dramatic. You can avoid by ignoring a hurtful comment or quickly changing the subject when conversation begins to threaten. Another way to avoid is to place the responsibility for an issue back on your boss. A third way to withdraw is to use a simple response of "I'm looking into the matter," with the hopes that the boss will forget the issue.

The avoidance strategy is frequently used in large bureaucracies that have too many policies. Rather than tackling the conflict, you simply blame it on "policy." If you lack self-confidence in your communication abilities, you may hope the problem just disappears. However, following the dictum, "never complain, never explain," usually doesn't work in the long run. In fact, withdrawal has been negatively associated with knowledge of the boss's feelings and attitudes; open, upward communication; perceived helpfulness of the subordinate; and strength of the planning relationship. Thus, avoiding conflict with the boss doesn't usually make things better in critical managerial areas.[iv]

Managing Conflict with the Boss and with Peers: Accommodate

The second type of conflict resolution is accommodating. You try to deal with conflict by giving in, hoping to make everyone happy. When using this approach, you emphasize maintaining relationships with bosses and coworkers, and you de-emphasize achieving productive goals. Since you are aiming for others' acceptance, you often give in to their desires in areas that conflict with your own. You use this style if you believe confrontation is destructive.

Typical attempts to accommodate may include such things as calling for a coffee break at a tense moment, breaking tension by cracking a joke, saying "you're right" when they're not, or engaging in some ritual show of togetherness such as an office birthday party. Since these efforts are likely to reduce feelings of conflict, they are better than simple avoidance. But handling conflict by giving in will probably have short-range effects. Just because someone does not experience a hostile or negative feeling does not mean the real cause of the conflict is resolved. In fact, accommodating is a camouflage approach that can break down at any time and create barriers to progress. Research has found that managers in low- or medium-performing organizations accommodate to reduce conflict more often than managers in high-performing organizations do.

In addition, accommodating hurts open communication with the boss and with participation in goal setting. Think of your latest performance review with your boss. Did you give in to the judgments of your work quality without discussion or pushback? If so, did the boss think you had accepted the judgments as fair and true? How did you feel afterward—motivated to work harder? Probably not.

Managing Conflict with Bosses and with Peers: Compromise

Compromise, the third strategy for conflict resolution up and across the ladder, assumes that half a loaf is better than none. Since compromise provides some gain for both sides rather than a unilateral victory or loss, you might judge this approach to be better than the other strategies just discussed.

Compromise is used when one of two conditions exists: (1) neither person thinks he/she can force their way on the other person or (2) one or both people believes winning may not be worth the cost in money, time, or energy. Compromise is often highly related to negotiating, which is a legitimate conflict resolution strategy in today's workplace. Compromising may make both parties think they won, but they may also both feel like losers. A negative overtone may develop in the working relationship, and any sense of trust may break down. While both people probably entered the negotiations with a cooperative attitude, a sense of competition may be the final outcome.

A second concern with compromise is that the person with the most information has the better position, usually the person who has a better network. This power of information may restrict open communication, often resulting in a lopsided compromise. A third factor is the principle of the least-interested party: The party that has the least interest in the outcome is the more powerful person in the negotiations. As a result, a coworker who has little concern about your welfare or the team's welfare may have the most influence in a compromise.

Managing Conflict with Subordinates: Force

The previous sections described traditional ways to approach conflict upward, that is, between you and your boss, and horizontally, between you and your peers at the same level of power. But what about conflict down the ladder, when you are experiencing conflict with your subordinates?

You use force when you need to meet production goals at all costs, without concern for the needs or acceptance of your subordinates or team.

Losing is destructive because you think it reduces status, seems weak, and fosters a poor image. You must win no matter what, because winning gives you a sense of excitement and achievement. Not surprisingly, forcing is the number one conflict resolution strategy that U.S. managers use.

The forcing strategy will probably cause later conflicts, however. To see the negative effect this style may have, just think about the language managers use to describe conflict: beat the opposition, battle, fight, conquer, coerce, smash, nuke. Such language and imagery can result in long-lasting, emotional wounds.

While force can resolve immediate disputes, the long-term effects will probably include a loss of productivity. Forcing in conflict situations is negatively associated with adequacy of planning, helpfulness of the supervision, and participation in goal setting. The major result of forcing is that your employees are reluctant to carry out orders because they think that the ultimate resolution of the conflict will put them on the losing side of a win–lose position.

Interestingly, while little doubt exists that forcing has limited use, managers consider forcing to be their favorite backup strategy for dealing with conflict. Immediate compliance is misperceived as a long-term solution in these cases.

Managing Conflict with Anyone: Collaborate.

So far, it may seem that no totally acceptable, productive strategy exists to manage conflict. I've discussed everything in terms of loss. Fortunately, this is not the case. Collaborating, the fifth strategy, is a win–win strategy for conflict. This complex and highly effective style requires skillful, strategic managerial communication, but it reaps a big dividend; thus, the remainder of this chapter centers on this strategy. Let's first describe the win–win strategy and then examine specific ways to use it.

The key to this strategy is that it follows a mutual problem-solving approach rather than a combative one. In contrast to managers who use accommodating, avoiding, compromising, or forcing, managers who collaborate assume that a high-quality, mutually acceptable solution is possible. Everyone directs energies toward defeating the problem and not each other.

Here are the five steps in the collaboration process:

1. *Define the problem.* The problem definition must be specific. A statement of the problem in a conflict situation is usually much more difficult than it seems, and most people jump to solutions before they clearly define the problem. Because of this, our inclination is to state the problem as a solution rather than as a goal, which results in ambiguous communication. The outcome may be increased conflict. One helpful strategy is to write out the problem statement clearly, so everyone can see it and agree on it. Or you can agree on a problem stated as a question. State goals in the form of group goals rather than your own goals.

2. *Analyze the problem.* Again, most people want to skip this step. After all, they may argue, they live with the problem. What is the point of spending more time wallowing in it? The answer is that by exploring the depths of the problem, by looking at its history, causes, effects, and extent, you can later come up with a solution that addresses more than symptoms, one that is more than a bandage. The analysis will address the root cause of the problem, thus improving the chances of being successful.

3. *Brainstorm alternatives.* Everyone involved in the conflict should offer potential solutions. One idea may stimulate other ideas. The more you communicate in an open, trusting environment, the greater the potential for finding effective solutions. Trust, of course, evaporates when an idea is criticized during a brainstorming session. As soon as someone says, "That's a terrible idea. It'll never work," who would be willing to take the risk of coming up with another idea? Make sure that you don't judge ideas prematurely.

4. *Develop criteria for a good solution.* These criteria, or standards, may already be in place and available. Other times, your boss will tell you what a good solution must look like. Occasionally, you and/or your team are allowed to develop your own criteria. The most common criteria for a good solution are:
   • It must be cheap.
   • It must be easy to do.
   • It must call for using resources already on hand.
   • It must be legal.
   • It must be in line with the company's mission or values.

5. *Evaluate the brainstormed alternatives using the criteria.* This is really the easiest step. By this time, you have reached agreement on the problem, and everyone has had a say about possible solutions. The best solution will appear naturally because it is the brainstormed alternative that matches your list of criteria.

Steps in the Collaboration Process:

1. Define the problem
2. Analyze the problem
3. Brainstorm solutions
4. Develop criteria for a good solution
5. Find the best match

You might be asking, if collaborating is the best all-around strategy for resolving conflict, why don't we do it more often? The simple answer is that this process calls for two prerequisites: time and ability. You can't count on reaching consensus on a solution right away. Hearing everyone out takes time and patience, commodities that are rare in today's workplace. Secondly, the people have to know how to collaborate; they must be familiar with, and be willing to follow, the five steps described above.

Once I had a graduate student who managed the third shift in a manufacturing company. After attending my evening class from 6:00 to 9:00 p.m., Rob would head off to work from 11:00 p.m. to 7:00 a.m. Before class one evening, Rob told me that two of his subordinates had been locked in conflict for some time over a tools issue, and so he had tried using the collaborative strategy that I had taught in class. "How did it go?" I asked eagerly. Rob reported, "It didn't work." He had put his employees into the break room and said, "Come out when you two have reached an agreement." After an hour, they had returned to the line, saying they'd worked it out, but Rob said they hadn't used the process he had learned in class. When I asked what they had used, he told me, "Seniority." The worker who had been on the job longer got his way.

This example demonstrates the importance of training people on the steps in the collaboration strategy for conflict resolution. It's based on how we think when we are trying to rationally solve a problem, but participants must know and stick to the steps in the process for it to work.

Summary

To help you "get it done," this chapter focuses on strategies for managing conflict. Conflict is inevitable in the workplace, and it's even more powerful a factor when the workforce is diverse. You will be able to successfully deal with conflict by following the steps described here: read the situation to identify the source of the conflict, recognize whether the conflict is constructive or destructive, select the right strategy out of the toolbox, and then apply it. Table 8.1 will help you choose the right conflict resolution strategy.

Table 8.1 When to Use Each Conflict Resolution Strategy

Conflict Resolution Strategy	When It Works Best	Result
Avoiding	• There's little chance you'll get your way • The potential damage of addressing the conflict outweighs the benefits of resolution • People need a chance to cool down • Others are in a better position to resolve the conflict • The problem will go away by itself	I lose You lose
Accommodating	• Preserving harmony is important • Personal antagonism is the major source of conflict • The issue itself is unsolvable • You care more about the relationship than getting your way	I lose You win
Compromising	• Two opponents are equal in power • Temporary settlements on complex issues are needed • Opponents do not share goals • Forcing or problem solving won't work	I half win, half lose You half win, half lose
Forcing	• Quick, decisive action is needed, as in a crisis • A rule has to be enforced • You know you're right • You must protect yourself	I win You lose

(Continued)

Table 8.1 When to Use Each Conflict Resolution Strategy (Continued)

Conflict Resolution Strategy	When It Works Best	Result
Collaborating	• Both sets of concerns are too important to be compromised • It is important to work through hard feelings • Commitment to the resolution is important • A permanent solution is desired	I win You win

Endnotes

i. L.A. Erbert (2014). "Antagonistic and Non-Antagonistic Dialectical Contradictions in Organizational Conflict," *International Journal of Business Communication* 51, no. 2, pp. 138–58.

ii. L. Putnam, S. Wilson (1988). "Argumentation and Bargaining Strategies as Discriminators of Integrative and Distributive Outcomes," in *Managing Conflict: An Interdisciplinary Approach,* ed. A. Rahim (New York, NY: Praeger Publishers), pp. 121–141.

iii. R. Hoffman, E. Harburg, N.R.F. Meier (1962). "Differences and Disagreements as Factors in Creative Problem-Solving," *Journal of Abnormal and Social Psychology* 64, no. 2, pp. 206–24.

iv. W.A. Donohue, M.E. Diez, R.B. Stahl (1983). "New Directions in Negotiations Research," in *Communication Yearbook* 7, ed. R.N. Bostrom (Beverly Hills, CA: Sage Publications), pp. 249–79.

CHAPTER 9

Strategies for Detecting Deception

As we've said, "getting it done" is all about daily workplace interactions that you as a manager need to navigate. So far in this section we've talked about how to give clear directives (Chapter 6) and how to give corrective feedback (Chapter 7). Continuing our examination of tough communication challenges that you face every day, Chapter 8 looked at conflict and offered five strategies for managing it. This chapter focuses on another communication challenge—figuring out when someone is lying to you.

The Importance of Nonverbal Cues

How often do you find yourself wondering whether the data your employees work with are accurate? While the data set out in a report can usually be tested objectively, information you get from face-to-face interactions such as disciplinary and pre-employment screening interviews can't immediately be checked for accuracy. Fortunately, some nonverbal cues can help you decide whether what people are saying to you is true.

As you read in Chapter 4, nonverbal cues usually reinforce or repeat verbal ones and are used to reduce the uncertainty in communication. On the other hand, nonverbal cues might contradict the verbal ones they accompany. When you are listening to someone and what they say contradicts how they look, which do you believe? For instance, if a speaker says, "I'm delighted to be here," while she mops her brow, wads up her notes, and gulps water, do you really think she's "delighted"?

Similarly, when a manager says, for example, that the customer is always first, but then reprimands subordinates for taking too much time with a customer, the manager's actions are what the employees believe—not the words. As you read in Chapter 5, inconsistency between verbal and nonverbal messages appears deceptive and generates distrust. On the other hand, consistency between words and behavior builds trust.

When what you say contradicts how you look, people believe how you look.

Contradictory nonverbal cues that betray deception are called *leakage*. When someone is lying, certain types of nonverbal cues often escape despite the speaker's attempts to control them. The subconscious apparently betrays the speaker through this nonverbal leakage. Listeners and observers read and interpret these signals, often subconsciously. That, in a nutshell, is how you can learn to spot nonverbal signs of deception.

Several patterns of nonverbal behavior crop up when someone is lying. Since you can control some sources of nonverbal cues better than others—for example, blushing is a physiological effect of lying—we will focus on signals that are difficult for you to consciously control. These include movement, dress, personal space, and voice.

Misinterpretation of Nonverbal Cues

Before exploring ways to tell from the nonverbal signals whether someone is lying, a word of caution is in order. Remember from Chapter 4 that nonverbal behavior usually *suggests* meaning rather than having a one-to-one connection with a specific word or idea. A nonverbal cue might actually mean something different than you think it means for many reasons, such as cultural differences, and a gesture might be motivated by something other than what you assumed.

Here's an example of how easily gestures can be misinterpreted. Let's say you're wrapping up a meeting with the team at your company's Honduras site, and you decide to signal that you are happy about the outcome, so you connect your thumb and forefinger in a circle and hold the other fingers straight, indicating the word *okay*. Others in the room react emotionally, thinking you are not happy with the meeting at all, because people in much of Latin America may consider this gesture to be obscene.

Eye contact is another example of nonverbal behavior that is easily misinterpreted. The mainstream U.S. business culture equates direct eye contact with honesty. We think that speakers who don't look at us while speaking have "shifty eyes" and are hiding something. We trust people who will "look us in the eye." Many other cultures, however, think that direct eye contact is vulgar and disrespectful. Within the U. S., eye contact patterns differ among African-Americans, Native Americans, and Anglo-Americans. Patterns differ between men and women in the U. S. too—women look less while speaking and more while listening than men do. Power and status often affect eye contact patterns, since gaze indicates dominance in the U.S. business world.

In Asian countries workers typically gaze downward when interacting with their bosses to indicate respect for authority. Japanese audiences may actually close their eyes to indicate they are listening intently to a speech. In the U. S., if an audience's eyes are closed, the speaker has put them to sleep.

Having said that nonverbal cues are always important in daily communication, that nonverbal cues are easily misinterpreted, and that some nonverbals can be controlled better than others, we are ready to discuss strategies for detecting deception.

Position

To detect possible nonverbal signs of deception, it is important to be in the right place. Often, employees sit behind desks or stand behind equipment, so significant cues are hidden. The face, always likely to be visible, can be a poor source of deception cues (although hand-to-face contacts are valuable cues). When possible, position the other person in an open chair facing you, or standing where you can see them full on. Nonverbal signs from the hands, trunk, legs, or feet then will be more evident.[i]

Baseline Nonverbal Cues

The basic theory is that deception cues are behaviors that are different from normal nonverbal cues. Therefore, you need to know what behavior is normal for that individual—their *baseline*. Researchers have found that when observers see someone giving honest answers before giving dishonest answers, the observers' ability to detect the dishonesty increases significantly compared to when there was no behavioral baseline. According to psychologist Paul Ekman of the University of California—San Francisco, you don't detect dishonesty by looking for the lie, but by noticing a change in behavior that suggests a person is nervous when he or she shouldn't be.[ii]

The individual's baseline is also invaluable because one person might behave differently from others in the same circumstances. A baseline allows you to tell if nervous behavior reflects the overall situation or if it's a reaction to the question you asked.

In a job interview, a baseline is relatively easy. At the opening, you should greet the applicant and make small talk, asking nonthreatening questions about the weather, their trip, or a big sports event. Once you've settled into the interview, begin asking questions about the résumé rather than jumping right into tougher questions. Watch for baseline nonverbal cues.

If you are investigating a safety violation or similar event on the job, your interrogation could use the same pattern. Small talk serves its traditional primary purpose of putting the other person at ease, and a secondary one of providing a baseline of nonverbal behavior.

Some typical nonverbal signs of deception, or variations from the baseline nonverbal behaviors, are summarized in Table 9.1, with a discussion of each one following.

Table 9.1 Nonverbal Signs of Deception

Unexpected movements and gestures
Manipulation of clothing
Increase of personal space
Misleading artifacts
Vocal variations

Movements and Gestures

Gestures and trunk movements are probably the most valuable nonverbal signs of deception. Perhaps the most common deception-related gestures are the hand-to-face movements, and the most common of these is the mouth cover. More subtle is the single finger to the mouth, the moustache stroke, or the nose rub. Other gestures suggesting deception are nail biting and lip biting. Hiding the hands by putting them in pockets or pulling shirtsleeves down to the fingertips are a sign that the person is "hiding" something more than their hands.

Conversational gestures tend to vary as well when an individual is being dishonest. Generally, when individuals are comfortable and giving honest responses, their gestures are open and outward. During deception, most people both limit their gestures and keep them closer to the body. Smiling decreases and the frequency of gestures used to illustrate conversational points slows down, but the gestures suggesting deception increase. One of these is the hand shrug. Researchers have found that when individuals are lying, they will shrug their hands—turning the palms up from palms down position—twice as frequently as when they are telling the truth. This signal suggests a subconscious pleading for the listener to believe what they are saying.[iii]

Some authorities also claim that an increase in leg and foot movements may indicate deception. Foot tapping, leg rocking while the legs are crossed, and frequent shifts in leg posture are examples of this kind of activity. A rhythmic "walking" motion with one crossed leg is a classic movement that suggests the person would like to walk away. Table 9.2 summarizes movements of different body segments that you should look for when trying to detect deception. But keep in mind the need to compare behavior with the baseline for the individual.

Table 9.2 Deceptive Movements

Body Segment	Movement	Interpretation
Head	Shifting, darting eyes	Uncertain; lying
	Eyebrows up	Challenging
	Head down	Defensive
Trunk, shoulders	Leaning away	Skeptical
	Slouched	Low self-esteem
	Shrunken chest	Threatened
Hands, arms	Touching self, stroking hair	Nervous; anxious
	Repetitive movements	Lying; unsure of self
	Hand over mouth while speaking	Wants to escape
	Arms crossed	Protective; closed
	Hands on hips	Challenging, combative
	Hands in pockets	Secretive
	Palms hidden	Distrustful
	Pointing	Aggressive
	Clenched hands; picking cuticle	Needs reassurance

After this quick review of deception movements, you may wonder whether there are others. Yes, signs of deception are not confined to the body. They can involve dress, space, artifacts, and voice. These cues are discussed next.

Manipulation of Clothing

Regarding dress, nonverbal leakage mainly shows up in the way people handle their clothes, which may suggest that they feel threatened by a certain question or topic. An employee may suddenly close and button his or her jacket or begin to tug nervously at a pants leg or skirt hem. Some people, particularly women, may pull their sleeves down over their hands or tuck their clothes tighter around their laps. This may betray a fear of having some deception uncovered. Other signals include straightening or tugging at the collar, smoothing the tie, picking at lint, or rubbing at a spot.

Personal Space

The distance that someone keeps from others as well as their relation to the surrounding environment may be a rich source of deception cues. An employee or job applicant might shift the chair's position or might suddenly lean back on the chair's rear legs. Moving away from you may show a lack of cooperativeness, or it might be a feeble attempt to put distance between the two of you by changing the environment. Typically, as you have probably noticed, when a person in a conversation physically backs up, the other person comes closer. In stand-up conversations, if the employee or applicant is giving a deceptive response to your question, they may lean back or step back and try to prevent you from bridging the gap by "blocking" with a piece of furniture, an object, or even by folding the arms across the chest.

An employee or applicant who has been relaxed may shift under pressure. For example, deception may leak out when the person suddenly crosses the arms and legs and leans back. The vulnerable forward posture is less comfortable when facing the fear of discovery. The person may also try to erect *signal blunders* to hide behind. These may be such subtle activities as placing a purse or briefcase in the lap as a barrier. On the other hand, an employee or applicant might "open up" physically during a response, suggesting openness and honesty.

Misleading Artifacts

Personal possessions in the workplace and the physical environment itself offer cues, and they can be manipulated to create an intended impression. Some people will meticulously decorate their offices or cubicles in an attempt to manage the perceptions of their visitors. Although many of these decorations can reflect honest identity claims, some can be strategic and even deceptive.[iv] How many times has a car salesperson lured you back to their office, where an overabundance of religious symbols is on display? How about cute kiddie photos? Such artifacts seem to say, "You can trust me. I'm a person of faith. I'm family oriented. I would never give you a raw deal." Excessively showcasing awards, plaques, framed certificates, and photos taken with celebrities on a "brag wall" is another common attempt at self-promotion. Personal effects in the office can serve as clues to who the real person is, but you should interpret their significance carefully.

The following true story illustrates the importance of artifacts in the workplace. Once I was hired to coach the owner of a freight company on her interpersonal communication skills. She told me that she had inherited the business from her late husband, and she was having difficulty getting the employees to take her seriously. Everyone ignored her directives, she complained.

As she talked, I glanced around her office. I saw piles of clothing and shoes, foam plastic clamshells of leftover take-out meals, half-empty coffee cups, stacks of files and papers. The chairs and tables were covered with clutter. When her phone rang, she had difficulty finding it on the desk. No wonder people didn't listen to her. She didn't seem to be able to manage her office environment, let alone her business. I helped her realize that if she wanted her employees to think of her as a leader, not only did she have to look like, talk like, and act like a leader, but also her office had to look like a leader's office.

Voice

Voice is another rich source of cues. Everyone's voice is unique. That's how you can tell who is calling just by hearing them say "hello" on the phone. Just as we learned in our review of movement and gestures, any unexpected changes from baseline behaviors can indicate deception. Furthermore, there are patterns of vocal style that we come to expect from people, and when those patterns vary from the norm, we may become rightfully suspicious.

> When what you say contradicts how you sound, people believe how you sound.

Think of the people in your workgroup. Because you meet regularly, you've come to expect that Donna speaks first, speaks fast, and speaks loudly about every agenda item. When someone tries to interrupt, she keeps talking, faster and louder. On this particular agenda item, however, which is relevant to her team's current project, she has remained strangely silent. When you ask for the relevant data, she hesitates before responding and then rambles about how hard her team is working. You follow up by asking whether there will be a problem meeting the project's deadline. Slowly, again, and with an increasingly strident pitch, she says, "Of course not. My people have always come through, haven't they? Don't you remember the Croft account fiasco that we narrowly avoided just because my team pulled together over that long weekend?" Should you be worried? Probably.

Most relevant in detecting deception are the pitch, tone, and volume of the voice. Researchers have found that vocal pitch rises measurably in deceptive responses. While observers frequently could not say why they labeled such a response as deceptive, they knew it was, and research instruments revealed the pitch difference.[v]

The start and length of a response are also clues to deception. Authorities have long known that deceptive answers have a slower start than honest ones. In addition, deceptive answers are likely to be longer and less specific than honest ones. The deceiver may be attempting to fill in the gap with needless material. Some see length as an attempt to make a deceptive answer more elaborate and thus more convincing than the deceiver knows it is. The answer's length may also reflect the pauses and hesitations needed as the employee or applicant stumbles through an answer.

Vocal Aspects of Deception:

- Pitch
- Tone
- Volume
- Onset
- Duration

Summary

"Getting it done" means tuning in to the nonverbal messages that coworkers, subordinates, bosses, and applicants communicate. When managers interact with employees and potential employees, nonverbal elements are the source of most of the message. While not everything communicated nonverbally is done so consciously or intentionally, the unintentional signals may be as valid as the intentional ones and are potentially more useful in deciding whether the person is being honest or deceptive.

Keep in mind, though, the value of establishing a behavioral baseline for each person in specific situations. Then simply watch and listen for sudden deviations. In addition, if you suspect deception, use that as a sign of caution and the need to investigate further. Don't jump to conclusions or take your perceptions as the final word. Remember to factor in cultural differences and the possibility that a particular conversation topic has caused the employee to become self-conscious, tense, or emotional.

Endnotes

i. J.L. Waltman (1983). "Nonverbal Interrogation: Some Applications," *Journal of Police Science and Administration* 11, no. 2, p. 167.

   ii. J. Gammage (2006, January 29). "Good Liars May be Wired Differ-ently," *Houston Chronicle,* p. 2D.

  iii. C.J. McClintock, Raymond G. Hunt (1975). "Nonverbal Indicators of Affect and Deception in Interview Situations," *Journal of Applied Psychology* 5, no. 3, p. 420.

   iv. S. Gosling (2008). *Snoop: What Your Stuff Says about You* (London, UK: Profile Books), p. 13.

    v. P. Ekman, W. Friesen, K.R. Scherer (1976). "Body Movement and Voice Pitch in Deception Interaction," *Semiotica* 16, no. 11, p. 26.

PART 4

Get Ahead

CHAPTER 10

Trends in the Global Work Environment

Let's review for a moment. This book is designed to help you "get along, get it done, and get ahead" at work. Chapter 3 in Part One introduced you to the Sequence for Success model that is at the heart of the book (Figure 10.1). The model illustrates how interpersonal communication behavior leads to strong work relationships, which build loyalty, satisfaction, and commitment. These positive emotions are prerequisites for maximum performance and organizational success.

In Part Two, you read about strategies for "getting along." You learned best practices for communicating up, down, and across the hierarchy. You were introduced to communication behaviors that will help you find out what's going on and what people are thinking. You also learned how to build trusting relationships that allow you to influence coworkers' actions.

In Part Three you read about strategies for "getting it done." You discovered best practices for communicating job expectations to your subordinates, giving feedback about how well they're doing, and presenting ways to improve. You learned strategies for managing conflict with the boss as well as conflict among subordinates. And you learned how to tell when someone is lying to you.

Now here we are at Part Four, ready to look into the future. In order to "get ahead" you first should tune in to major trends in the global work environment. Chapter 10 identifies four of these trends and offers ways to get onboard. Then you will know how to thrive in tomorrow's workplace, which is the subject of Chapter 11.

Figure 10.1 Sequence for Success.

Trends

You will want to consider four major trends in the global work environment as you manage your career: increasing reliance on technology, growing reliance on teams and collaboration, expanding workforce diversity, and heightened emphasis on ethics. Table 10.1 summarizes the trends and introduces implications for your success as a manager.

Table 10.1 Trends in Global Business and Implications for Managers

Trends	What to Do about It
Increasing reliance on technology	• Become media sensitive • Guide employees' use of technology
Increasing reliance on teams and collaboration	• Use social media/collaboration tools • Provide training
Increasing workforce diversity	• Learn another language • Create a welcoming culture
Increasing emphasis on ethics	• Have a formal code of conduct • Broadcast it to everyone

1. Increasing Reliance on Technology

If you spend as much time as most managers do reading and responding to email, texting your staff, blogging both internally and with external stakeholders, participating in webinars and virtual meetings, and compulsively checking your smartphone while sitting in traffic, you know that developments in technology will largely determine the future of business. In the words of Tom Friedman, columnist for the *New York Times* and winner of three Pulitzer Prizes, we have gone from a connected world to a hyperconnected world in the last 10 years.

Today, technology is an integral part of everyone's work life. The justification for our increasing reliance on technology is increased efficiency and productivity and improved communication. But technology is more than a beneficial tool; it's a force that must be constantly reassessed. Technology is not always good just because it's new. It's a thin line to walk, and it requires some creative thinking to stay balanced between technological advantage and overkill.

Advantages of technology:

- Increased efficiency
- Increased productivity
- Improved communication

Communication technology creates both advantages and disadvantages in organizations. Over-reliance on technology brings a danger of sensory overload, a decline in work relationships, and reduced opportunities for corrective feedback. Speaking of sensory overload, if you feel buried by email these days, just wait. By 2017 the majority of email traffic is predicted to come from business email rather than personal email. Business email will account for a whopping 132 billion emails sent and received per day. Personal email traffic, by contrast, is expected to decrease over the next few years, with individuals opting to use social media, instant messaging (IM), and texting to communicate with friends and families.[i]

Disadvantages of technology:

- Sensory overload
- Weak work relationships
- Reduced feedback

Despite the potential disadvantages of technology, networked organizations are the norm, mostly because they increase productivity and efficiency. The strategic decision for you is not whether to use technological channels but which channel is best for the situation and how to maximize its capabilities.

Media Sensitivity. As a manager, you can't simply rely on the channel you feel most comfortable with when communicating; you need to consider the impression the channel makes with your intended audience. Here is a true story that demonstrates this idea. Once there was an accounting department manager who relied exclusively on sticky notes for communicating with her subordinates, to the extent that she would silently enter a worker's cubicle, stick the note onto the computer monitor, and silently leave again, while the subordinate sat right there. How do you think the employees felt about the manager and her message?

You must decide when to use technology and when to speak face-to-face with your intended audience. Different situations and messages call for different channels, as illustrated in Table 10.2.

Table 10.2 Channel Options for Messages

Message Type	Message Example	Key Channel Characteristics	Channel Example
Sensitive	Condolence	Broad bandwidth Feedback mechanism Symbolic importance	Face-to-face
Negative	Layoff	Broad bandwidth Feedback mechanism	Face-to-face Videoconference
Complex	Procedure	Permanence Feedback mechanism	Multiple channels
Routine	Meeting reminder	Low cost Efficiency	Email Poster
Persuasive	Sales	Broad bandwidth Interactive Symbolic importance Feedback mechanism	Face-to-face Videoconference
Need for immediate response	Question	Feedback mechanism Speed	Text message Instant message Face-to-face
Informative	New product	Permanence Accessibility	Blog Email Newsletter

Why should you care about channel choice? Because it's a key to success. Several studies have identified a strong correlation between a manager's media sensitivity and managerial performance. When a task involved complex information or was highly emotional, for instance, effective managers were more inclined than were ineffective managers to use communication channels with a broad bandwidth, or capacity to carry information, such as face-to-face conversation.[ii] So if you want to be successful at work, become media sensitive.

Successful managers are media-sensitive managers.

Media sensitivity includes guiding your subordinates in the proper, ethical use of communication technology. For instance, IM is an official corporate communication tool for over one-fourth of U.S. companies. Employees use IM on their own in another 44 percent of companies, sometimes for personal as well as business-related communication. Yet 35 percent of companies don't have an official IM policy, risking breaches of confidentiality, viruses, and copyright infringement.[iii] New communication tools are constantly becoming available, requiring strategic decisions about their use. Your subordinates rely on you for training and for modeling ethical use of technology.

Media Surveillance. A second prediction about communication technology is that monitoring mechanisms will become increasingly sophisticated. Surveillance methods are developing right along with innovations in technology. For example, federal law enforcement and national security offices have sweeping authority to monitor Internet communications, including encrypted emails, social networking websites, and peer-to-peer software such as Skype. In the United States, phone and broadband networks are already required to have government interception capabilities under a 1994 law called the Communications Assistance to Law Enforcement Act.

The business sector is following the example of government surveillance policies by developing technologies that allow them to eavesdrop on employees. Electronic monitoring systems allow employers to gather very detailed information about how their employees spend their time at work.[iv] Companies monitor employees for many reasons. These include:

- Preventing lawsuits
- Reducing the misuse of company resources
- Protecting intellectual property[v]

Companies have invested in technology that can do much more than block access to certain Internet sites. They frequently have the ability to record every key stroke ever typed on a worker's computer (even ones that have been deleted).

Assume your technology use at work is being monitored.

Monitoring by employers is widespread and supported by the courts. A survey of more than 700 companies by the Society for Human Resource Management (SHRM) found that:

- Almost 75 percent of the companies monitor their workers' Internet use.
- 43 percent monitor their workers' email.
- 45 percent monitor phone use.
- 45 percent track content, keystrokes, and time spent at the keyboard.[vi]

Furthermore, employers may not alert employees to the fact that they are watching. Only two states, Delaware and Connecticut, require employers to notify employees of monitoring. According to a recent American Management Association survey:

- 17 percent of employers do not inform workers that the company is monitoring content, keystrokes, and time spent at the keyboard.
- 16 percent do not let employees know the company reviews computer activity.
- 29 percent do not alert employees to email monitoring.[vii]

Your employees should realize that any time spent using technology at work should be limited to work-related activities. Further, any messages they send or receive at work should be appropriate for anyone to read. In 2010, in its first ruling on the privacy rights of employees who send messages on the job, the Supreme Court unanimously agreed that supervisors may read through subordinates' text messages if they suspect that work rules are being violated. So warn your people to be on their best behavior and to think twice before doing something even questionable while on the job.

2. Increasing Reliance on Teams and Collaboration

Job trends research confirms that collaboration and teamwork are among the top 10 critical work skills for the future.[viii] In fact, 90 percent of all

U.S. businesses and 100 percent of Fortune 500 companies use some form of group structure already. Their need for collaboration lies in the complexity and interdependence of tasks, which make it difficult for one person to have enough information to make decisions and solve problems in today's organizations.

It's easy to see why teams have been adopted as a key work structure in contemporary organizations. Today's workplace is fast paced and intense. The traditional management hierarchy is often clumsy and slow in responding to changes in the marketplace. So many organizations have replaced a bureaucratic hierarchy with flexible, cooperative, mission-driven teams led by managers who expect their subordinates to participate fully in the task or project at hand.

If you are this kind of manager, you encourage collaboration and group loyalty among your team members every day. The focus is on using two-way communication tools to encourage input and keep everyone informed, thereby creating a sense of community and a collaborative culture.

Virtual teams use social media tools to support collaboration.

When your subordinates are on the road, geographically scattered, or on flexible schedules, communication challenges are even greater. If face-to-face interactions are not practical, you can use social enterprise tools such as Facebook at Work, Yammer, or Jive to connect people. Streaming video and IM are well suited to building community.

A 2013 survey of 651 organizations in a range of industries and global regions found that the majority of employers (56 percent) use social media to communicate with employees on topics such as organizational culture, team building, change management, and innovation. Furthermore, 70 percent of the survey respondents agreed that the use of internal social business/collaboration tools had a positive impact on employee productivity.[ix] The more managers use these tools, the more adept they become at fostering collaboration. When employees connect, either in person or through technologies, they can establish dialogues and collaboration rather than relying on top-down communication. The manager of the future must know how to support collaboration.

Leading Teams. Managing teams calls for special leadership skills. First, it's important to select team members who communicate information freely and honestly. Once your team is in place, here are some other strategies that will support collaboration:

- *Be a facilitator.* Managing teams is less about supervising than it is about motivating members to do their best. Avoid the tendency to micromanage once you have defined the team's objectives and responsibilities.
- *Support the team.* Provide resources, run interference, and resolve internal conflicts. Give them all the information they need, and more, to encourage trust. Remember that people cannot work in a vacuum.
- *Delegate.* Managers occasionally have trouble admitting that they cannot do it all. Instead of trying to manage every aspect of a meeting or project, trust members to perform their assigned tasks. This trust also builds respect for you as a leader and maintains morale.
- *Seek diversity.* Heterogeneous groups experience more conflict but often produce higher-quality results than homogeneous groups. Stress the importance of collaboration, flexibility, and openness toward unfamiliar viewpoints and work styles.[x]

Tips for managing work teams:

- Be a facilitator
- Support the team
- Delegate
- Seek diversity

In teams or work groups that are culturally diverse, you may have to deal with communication difficulties and language barriers, which decrease cohesion. Be sure your people put teammates at ease by respecting the conventions of each culture. Writing styles, for example, differ across cultures. A direct, concise email may be standard in the United States, but Japanese recipients may consider it rude and vulgar. That's why an email I recently sent to a colleague at a Japanese university began with, "The local cherry blossoms are particularly beautiful this spring."

Fluency may be a roadblock for transnational team members communicating in English. As the team leader, you can build in more time during teleconferences and perhaps hire translators. Nonverbal behavior also varies from culture to culture, as you read in Chapter 4. For example, in the United States, business professionals usually shake hands when they "seal a deal," but unrelated men and women are forbidden to touch in Islamic countries. Videoconferencing tools allow your team to see and hear each other's nonverbal cues including posture, facial expression, and voice tone, yet the risk of misunderstanding remains strong. As a manager, you must decide whether these more expensive methods of communication are worth the attempt to reduce the assumptions and barriers involved. Cultural diversity training can reduce the likelihood of misunderstandings and blunders among your team.

3. Increasing Workforce Diversity

A third trend that will impact your success as a manager is the expanding diversity of the workforce. As your subordinates, peers, and bosses become more diverse, your communication skills will become more important than ever.

Types of Diversity. The data confirm what we have all already noticed in our own organizations—diversity is a reality along the dimensions of gender, age, education, and culture. Even in Silicon Valley, where high-tech firms were once known as bastions of white and Asian men, efforts are being made to attract more women, Latinos, and African-Americans. Why? Because companies with diversity tend to be more creative and more profitable. Varied perspectives help them design products and services that have global appeal.

You may be especially sensitive to issues of age diversity if you supervise workers older than you are. The percentage of those over 65 who have remained in the workforce has been rising steadily since the 1990s. The U.S. Census Bureau projects the portion of those 65 and older who are working will grow to 23 percent by 2022. Astoundingly, almost 20 percent of 70 to 74 year olds are currently still working. And it's likely that they will want you to interact with them respectfully, just because of their age and experience. Since the payoff of a diverse workforce depends not on the diversity itself but on promoting a sense of belonging, you must use tact when managing people who may be your parents' (or grandparents') ages.

Culturally Sensitive Communication. Despite the fact that diverse workforces are the norm, a 2014 Towers Watson Global Workforce Study shows that only about half of today's managers are viewed as effective by their subordinates when it comes to their skill at listening to different points of view and working across cultural differences. [xi] Clearly the gap must be closed. The strategies described in Parts Two and Three of this book will help you develop a welcoming culture that values individuals regardless of skin, intellect, talents, gender, or years. As a manager, you must be able to connect with others in a deep and direct way and develop relationships that will bridge differences.

> **DIVERSITY =**
> **D**ifferent **I**ndividuals **V**aluing **E**ach other **R**egardless of **S**kin, **I**ntellect, **T**alents, or **Y**ears

Bridging differences takes social and emotional intelligence, as you read in Chapter 4. Cross-cultural competence involves awareness of differences and the ability to capitalize on those differences. Misunderstandings and communication breakdowns may also be due to differences in the degree of directness, appropriate subjects for conversation, touch, loudness and pitch, even silence. As a Yankee living in

Texas, I've had firsthand experience with cultural differences regarding proximity. At first my students, both male and female, surprised me by hugging me in greeting whenever I saw them on campus. Because it makes me uncomfortable, I advised them that where I come from, students don't hug their professors. But they just laughed, pointing out that I'm not in Chicago anymore. So I devised a scheme of hugging from the side to minimize the invasion of my personal space without insulting them.

Linguistic skills strongly affect cultural awareness. In her autobiography, U.S. Supreme Court Justice Sonia Sotomayor describes her struggles as a child in the South Bronx—she spoke only Spanish at home but attended classes taught only in English. Sotomayor argues that language is "a code of the soul" that unlocks the music, poetry, history, and literature of a culture, "but it is also a prison." Teachers lacking knowledge of Spanish language and culture, for example, didn't realize that Hispanic kids who looked down when scolded were doing so out of respect, as they'd been taught. This nonverbal behavior only invited more scolding: "Look at me when I speak to you!"

Justice Sotomayor learned early "that things break down [when] people can't imagine someone else's point of view."[xii] Learning at least a little about another language is a practical way to improve interpersonal communication on the job. Beyond that, it's a way to continue your education and manage your career. Learning another language indicates that you are aware of and accept another culture's values, traditions, and world view.

Speech and language differences, nonverbal behavior such as eye contact, and facial expressions all complicate the communication process in cross-cultural situations. In summary, to improve your communication with culturally diverse workers:

- Check for possible language differences as the source of misunderstanding.
- Look for possible cultural sources of misunderstanding.
- Acknowledge your communication mistakes and correct them.
- Correct others' inappropriate communication behavior.

4. Heightened Emphasis on Ethics

If you paid any attention at all to the major corporate scandals in the early 21st century, you know how dangerous unethical behavior can be. Executives at Adelphia, Arthur Andersen, Enron, WorldCom, Martha Stewart Omnimedia, HealthSouth, and other corporations were charged with major ethics violations—accounting fraud, stock manipulation, obstructing justice, lying, and so on. Many of the accused executives were convicted, and some of their companies were even destroyed.

Publicized scandals have resulted in expanded concern for ethical standards in business. The Sarbanes-Oxley Act of 2002 requires companies to develop a code of ethics applicable to employees and directors. Today, 93 percent of the Fortune 100 companies publish a code of ethics or conduct or a values statement. Furthermore, 58 percent of the Fortune 100 companies that have a code of conduct extend it to vendors and contractor companies.

Sarbanes-Oxley also makes corporate leaders responsible for the unethical behavior of their employees—unless they can show that they provided adequate ethical training for them. As a result, 79 percent of the Fortune 100 companies require employee training on their code of ethics, with proof of completion.[xiii]

You face ethical dilemmas and temptations every day. Ethical issues range from corporate accounting practices to social media use by employees, harassment, and pay equity. We discussed the importance of trust and a positive communication climate in Chapter 5. Unfortunately, it's difficult to develop trust when so many blatant examples of mistrust occur and when you face conflicting ethical demands. The only way to build trust is to follow the practices of ethical communication.

> The only way to build trust is to follow the practices of ethical communication.

If your company has not developed a formal code of ethics, check to see whether your professional association has. For instance, the American Society for Quality specifies standards of behavior for quality management professionals. The Institute for Supply Management also developed a code of ethics relevant to supply chain managers' challenges. Alternatively, you can compose one for yourself and your work group, perhaps with input from your human resources and legal departments. The code should clarify expectations of employee conduct and state that you expect your people to recognize the ethical dimensions of corporate behavior and communication. Your code of conduct may be broad or specific regarding values, but at a minimum, it should address managerial communication and sensitivity to cultural differences. It should also spell out consequences of noncompliance with the standards. Finally, you should broadcast your code to all employees and check that they understand it.

My Code of Conduct. Let me give you a personal example of a code of conduct. I am a member of the Association of Professional Communication Consultants (APCC). APCC publishes its members' code of conduct on its website (www.consultingsuccess.org) that explains that:

> "... as professional communication consultants, we must promote the highest standard of ethics in dealing with clients, other consultants, and the global community in which we live and work. Members of the Association of Professional Communication Consultants have an obligation to maintain these standards of ethical conduct. In recognition of this obligation, members agree to abide by the following code of ethics in providing consulting services."

Following this opening statement, eight situations are listed. The situations are ones that communication consultants typically experience. For each situation, the code spells out expected standards of service. For example, here's situation #4:

> "In dealing with materials prepared by participants or the client company in a consulting program, the consultant agrees to
>
> a. Consider all materials participants provide to be confidential;

b. Request and receive written permission before using any participant materials outside the consulting situation, and then protect the anonymity of the client organization and of the specific individuals unless given prior permission to disclose those names."

The implication of this standard is that, when I come across a document in my consulting practice that exemplifies a business writing principle that I cover in my MBA course, I will only show that document to my university students as a "real" example after the client company has given permission. I will always sanitize it, too, so curious students can't figure out where it came from. Ethical practices overarch both of my professional worlds—consulting and teaching.

Summary

This chapter provides a look into the future. In order to "get ahead" managers should tune in to major trends in the global work environment. Four of these trends we identified and discussed are (1) increasing reliance on technology, (2) growing reliance on teams and collaboration, (3) expanding workforce diversity, and (4) heightened emphasis on ethics.

The justification for our increasing reliance on technology is increased efficiency and productivity, but technology has both advantages and disadvantages. When messages are sensitive, negative, nonroutine, and/or complex, face-to-face interactions may be preferable to technology. Messages generated and received at work should not be considered private or protected, as surveillance of employees' use of technology will continue to grow.

A second trend, growing emphasis on collaboration, calls for managerial ability to use social media as a way to share information, thereby building community, even in the presence of diversity.

A third trend, expanding gender, age, education, and cultural diversity in the workplace, requires that managers improve their sensitivity by becoming familiar with others' practices, principles, language, and preferences. Similarly, managers should help their subordinates develop diversity awareness through training.

A fourth trend toward heightened emphasis on ethics requires that managers create a code of conduct and broadcast it to subordinates, peers, and other stakeholders. Managers face ethical dilemmas and temptations every day, and the only way to maintain trust and integrity is to consistently follow an established code of behavior.

Endnotes

i. Radicati Group (2014). "Email Statistics Report, 2013–2017," Retrieved from http://www.radicati.com/wp/wp_content/uploads/2013/04/Email-Statistics-Report-2013-2017-Executive -Summary.pdf

ii. G.S. Russ, R. L. Daft, R. H. Lengel (1990). "Media Selection and Managerial Characteristics in Organizational Communications," *Management Communication Quarterly* 4, no. 2, pp. 151–75.

iii. "The Present (and Future) of Business Communications" (2005, July 25). *Accounting Web*, Retrieved from http://www .accountingweb.com

iv. H.J. Wen, D. Schwieger, P. Gershuny (2007). "Internet Usage Monitoring In the Workplace: Its Legal Challenges and Implementation Strategies," *Information Systems Management* 24, no. 2, pp. 185–96.

v. D. Elmuti, H.H. Davis (2006). Not worth the bad will. *Industrial Management* 48, no. 6, pp. 26–30.

vi. J.D. Lisa Guerin (n.d.). "Monitoring Employee Communications: Learn the Rules on Monitoring Email, Voicemail, Telephone Conversations, and Internet Use," Retrieved from http://www.nolo.com/legal-encyclopedia/monitoring-employee-communications-29853.html

vii. American Management Association (2014, June 2). "The Latest on Employee Surveillance," Retrieved from http://www.amanet.org/training/articles/The-Latest-on-Workplace-Monitoring-and-Surveillance.aspx

viii. Institute for the Future (2011). "Future Work Skills 2020" (Institute for the Future for the University of Phoenix Research Institute), Retrieved from www.iftf.org

ix. Towers Watson (2013). "Change and Communication ROI Study—The 10th Anniversary Report," Retrieved from www .towerswatson.com

x. L. Hughes (2004, January–February). "Do's and Don'ts of Effective Team Leadership," *WIB, Magazine of the American Business Women's Association,* p. 10.

xi. Towers Watson (2013).

xii. S. Sotomayor (2014). *My Beloved World* (New York, NY: Vintage Books), pp. 199, 123.

xiii. R. Rasberry (2013, March 15). "A Study of How Fortune 100 Companies Communicate Ethics, Governance, Corporate Responsibility, Sustainability, and Human Rights," Paper Presented at the Association for Business Communication-Southwestern U.S. Annual Conference, Albuquerque, NM.

CHAPTER 11

Strategies for Thriving in Tomorrow's Global Workplace

Part Four is all about taking care of your career. Chapter 10 identified four major trends for you to keep in mind when preparing yourself for success in tomorrow's global business environment:

1. Increasing reliance on technology
2. Increasing reliance on teams and collaboration
3. Increasing diversity in the workforce
4. Increasing emphasis on ethics

This chapter narrows the focus to what is arguably the toughest but most important strategy for success, developing your cultural sensitivity, and offers tools to help you reach that goal. Further, it presents ideas for developing cultural sensitivity among your subordinates or work team, so they, too, can be successful in a diverse workplace.

Self-Assessment Tools

Before you can reach your goal, you have to identify where you are now. Self-assessment can be an uncomfortable process, but it's the way forward.

The Diversity Awareness Continuum

Here is a quick and easy tool for determining your starting point in developing cultural sensitivity (Table 11.1). Read and react to each sentence in the left-hand column by putting an X in one of the middle column spaces that best reflects where you fit. Then draw your profile by connecting your Xs.

Table 11.1 Diversity Awareness Continuum

	1 2 3 4 5	
I don't know about the cultural norms of different groups in my organization.	__ __ __ __ __	I know about the cultural norms of different groups in my organization.
I don't hold stereotypes about other groups.	__ __ __ __ __	I admit my stereotypes about other groups.
I feel partial to, and more comfortable with, some groups than others.	__ __ __ __ __	I feel equally comfortable with all groups.
I gravitate toward others who are like me.	__ __ __ __ __	I gravitate toward others who are different from me.
I prefer managing a homogeneous team.	__ __ __ __ __	I prefer managing a multicultural team.
I feel that everyone is the same, with similar values and preferences.	__ __ __ __ __	I feel that everyone is unique, with different values and preferences.
I'm confused by the culturally different behaviors I see among staff.	__ __ __ __ __	I understand the cultural influences behind some of the behaviors I see among staff.
I get irritated when confronted by someone who does not speak English.	__ __ __ __ __	I show patience and understanding with limited English speakers.
I'm task focused and don't like to waste time chatting.	__ __ __ __ __	I find that more gets done when I spend time on relationships first.
I feel that newcomers to this society should comply with our rules.	__ __ __ __ __	I feel that both newcomers and their employer organizations need to change to fit together.

Now that you know the starting point, it's easy to find your end point or goal. The closer your line is to the right-hand column, the greater your awareness and sensitivity regarding diversity. The closer to the left-hand column, the less aware you may be about diversity-related issues. Your goal is to move closer to the right-hand column on each dimension.

Bennett's Model

Milton Bennett designed a six-stage developmental model of cultural sensitivity, reflected in Figure 11.1.

Development of Intercultural Sensitivity

Experience of difference

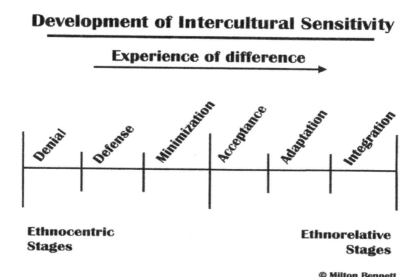

Ethnocentric Stages

Ethnorelative Stages

© Milton Bennett

Figure 11.1 Bennett's Model

Bennett's model provides another tool you might find useful for self-assessment. You will note that the first three stages in the model are "ethnocentric": *denial, defense,* and *minimization.* An example of a *denial* statement is, "No matter where you go, a smile will open all doors." At the second stage, *defense,* you are aware of differences but hostile toward other cultures, so you might say, "Our way is the right way." At the third stage, *minimization,* the differences you are aware of are superficial, so you might say something like, "When dining with my Chinese coworker, I'll use chopsticks."

Ethnocentric managers may acknowledge the existence of cultural differences but see their culture as the best in the world and looks down on others as inferior because they are different. For whatever reasons, the ethnocentric manager builds resentment rather than good relationships.

Stages of Ethnocentrism:

1. Denial
2. Defense
3. Minimization

On the other hand, Bennett identified three ethnorelative stages: *acceptance, adaptation,* and *integration* (Figure 11.1). An example of a statement by a manager at the *acceptance* stage is, "I see why we have belief differences," or "Differences are OK." If you are at Bennett's *adaptation* stage, you can empathize, so you might say something like, "I will adopt some aspects of a culture" or "Differences enhance the workplace." If you are at his *integration* stage, you have developed the ability to embrace and capitalize on differences. An example statement at this stage is, "We're not a melting pot. Let's go for the stir-fry."

Stages of Ethnorelativism:

1. Acceptance
2. Adaptation
3. Integration

An ethnorelativistic manager recognizes and respects cultural differences and finds ways to make the workplace amenable to all.[i] Try plotting your course for cultural sensitivity by identifying where you are on the following flowchart (Figure 11.2), which is based on Bennett's model.

How Culturally Competent Managers Behave

Let's say that through self-assessment and experience you've developed a level of cultural sensitivity. How does that manifest in your daily workplace behavior? In other words, how can you walk the talk? Michael Morris, a business professor at Columbia University, recognizes the common pitfalls managers face when trying to treat all employees fairly and respectfully. At one extreme, a manager may take the *universalist* approach, treating all employees the same. At the other extreme, a manager may take the *particularist* approach, adjusting the treatment according to the worker's culture. Both behaviors can have a negative effect on employees' perception of justice. "If justice issues are not well-managed in a diverse workplace, detrimental consequences ranging from poor morale and turnover to intergroup rivalry and balkanization may result."[ii]

Ethnocentricity ⬇	"Our way is the right way."
Awareness ⬇	"There may be another way."
Understanding ⬇	"I see why there are differences."
Acceptance ⬇	"Differences are OK."
Valuing ⬇	"Differences enhance the workplace."
Adoption ⬇	"I can pick what I like from a culture."
Multiculturalism	"We're not a melting pot. Let's go for the stir-fry."

Figure 11.2 Developing Cultural Sensitivity

Morris offers 10 ways managers can create a welcoming culture for diverse workers:

1. Rely on multiethnic strategies, not just on good intentions. For instance, you might implement a mentoring program to ensure that all employees develop important relationships.
2. Provide every employee constructive feedback so she or he may learn and grow.
3. Work to ensure that all cultural groups have access to opportunities.
4. Work to ensure that all cultural groups perceive that they are treated fairly.

5. Provide cultural competence training to supervisors who conduct performance reviews.
6. Monitor cultural boundaries to avoid intergroup competition.
7. Manage misunderstandings by making staff aware that cultural differences may be the root cause of clashes rather than personality differences.
8. Be sensitive to obstacles facing members of certain cultural groups and be flexible about performance evaluations to even the playing field.
9. Call on those with cultural expertise.
10. Include all employees and all cultures in diversity discussions.

In Chapter 7, I described a management tactic that I observed in a Houston manufacturing company. It bears revisiting because it exemplifies some of the strategies above. At this plant, the workforce was predominantly Vietnamese and the shift foreman was Mexican-American. The foreman recognized that in the Vietnamese culture the elders are greatly respected and obeyed, so he funneled his messages through the eldest workers rather than giving orders and corrective feedback directly to the younger employees. This two-step system was successful because the foreman acknowledged the cultural values of his Vietnamese subordinates.

Women, non-native Americans, and people of color represented approximately 73 percent of new entrants to the U.S. work force in 2012, and the percentage is steadily increasing. Some industries, however, still fail to attract and keep women and minorities. Why? When investigating the reasons that women and minorities leave jobs in the technology industry, researchers found that the most frequently cited reason was a hostile culture. Therefore, cultural sensitivity has taken on an urgency, both in hiring and keeping multicultural workers and in reaching the multicultural consumer market. Managing diversity is every manager's challenge.

Additional Managerial Competencies

Is there anything else that tomorrow's work environment will expect from its managers? Taking a broader perspective, we find that cultural sensitivity is fundamental, but additional competencies will contribute significantly to your success. Consider the following guidelines for survival in the global economy of the future:

1. *Accept ambiguity and uncertainty.* Respect the fact that change is constant, and you will have to be flexible.
2. *Reflect and think before acting.* As you manage multicultural teams and projects, be mindful and careful before acting or reacting. Sometimes, a thoughtless disregard of cultural values can create problems.
3. *Be creative and hardworking.* Effort, commitment, and innovative thinking are prerequisites for success. Be willing to take risks and keep trying.
4. *Be a lifelong learner.* Continuing education and professional development are worthwhile investments because growth ensures success for both you and your organization.[iii]

We know for sure that tomorrow's business environment will be different from that of today. Embracing change is not an option.

Your Improvement Plan

I imagine you nodding your head as you read the previous paragraphs. "Yes, these are all worthy goals," you are thinking. "I see the importance of cultural competence, emotional intelligence, embracing change, lifelong learning, etc. for my future success. I'm convinced. Now, how can I get there?" Simply, you will get there by taking one step at a time. Your personal improvement plan will work if it's action-oriented and ongoing.

Here's my suggestion: At the beginning of next month, sit down and write out three things you plan to do that month—one new action for professional improvement, one for personal improvement, and one for relationship improvement. Next to each new behavior write down in what situation and with whom you will do it. Table 11.2 shows you how to organize your personal improvement plan. It also might be helpful to look at the more elaborate work plan template in Appendix 3 at the back of this book. It shouldn't take you more than about 10 minutes to construct one.

Table 11.2 My Action Plan for the Month

	Goal	Who	When	Where	What I'll Say/Do
Professional					
Personal					
Relationship					

On the last day of next month, check your list to see how well you met those three goals. If you didn't succeed, try to figure out why not. Then, construct a new action plan consisting of three things you plan to do the following month, taking into account the roadblocks from last month. This system should keep you on track for developing competencies that are important for your career.

Developing Culturally Sensitive Employees

Once you've worked on your own cultural competence, it's time to address your subordinates' awareness. You don't have to send your staff overseas to develop their cultural sensitivity. There are several things you can do to help your workforce accept diversity.

"OK," you might say. "I'll send them to a cross-cultural communication training program." Yes, that's a good plan if a diversity training program is available. However, a recent study published by The Economist Intelligence Unit found that almost half (47 percent) of companies don't invest in such training, though they recognize the benefits of overcoming cultural and communication barriers.[iv]

Until companies acknowledge the need for culturally competent workers by committing more resources to formal training, managers can take some actions that will help employees develop cultural sensitivity.

- *Acknowledge the presence of culture differences.* Talk about differences in beliefs, values, goals, behaviors, and language. Try to understand and explain the reasons for these differences.
- *Insist on a respectful environment.* Be a role model by always using diversity-sensitive language yourself. Monitor others'

language, humor, and stories and point out the impact of
insensitive and offensive talk.

- *Promote the benefits of diversity.* Create and maintain
  heterogeneous teams. Be sure to consider age and gender
  as well as ethnicity and national origin when forming
  heterogeneous workgroups. Encourage multiple viewpoints
  during team meetings. Discourage groupthink and premature
  decision-making.

Ways to encourage employees' cultural competence:

- Acknowledge differences
- Insist on respect for differences
- Promote the benefits of diversity

The Bottom Line: Culturally Sensitive Managerial Communication

Developing cultural sensitivity in yourself and your people is an ongoing
process. The platform that fosters this process is daily interpersonal communication. A look to the future reveals a continued strong relationship
between effective interpersonal communication and organizational success. In fact, companies with highly effective communicators are three
and a half times more likely to significantly outperform their industry
peers than firms whose leaders are poor communicators.

What does "effective communication" mean in a culturally diverse
context? It begins with a deep understanding of the organization's culture
and the workers' cultures, because that knowledge allows leaders to create
messages that will drive worker behaviors toward the organization's goals.
A 2013 Towers Watson survey of 651 organizations worldwide found that
in highly effective organizations,

- 96 percent of managers act in support of the organization's
  vision and values
- 93 percent of managers deliver messages in a way that is
  meaningful for their work group

- 91 percent of managers work across cultural differences when determining procedures
- 90 percent of managers listen carefully to different points of view.[v]

Data published by a Project Management Institute study indicate even more behaviors that distinguish effective business communicators:

- They communicate frequently with their staff about goals, budgets, schedules, and business benefits.
- They communicate with sufficient clarity and detail.
- They use non-technical language.
- They tailor messages to different stakeholder groups.
- They use appropriate settings or media.[vi]

Remember the Sequence for Success model introduced in Chapter 3 and referred to throughout this book? The model illustrates how your daily communication leads to strong relationships, which lead to loyalty, satisfaction, and commitment. These emotional conditions lead to productivity and organizational success (Figure 11.3).

The model is a good place to end, because it captures the message I want to leave you with: tomorrow's managers will thrive during times of change if they are skillful communicators, emotionally intelligent, collaborative, and culturally sensitive. Following the Sequence for Success will enable you to use your effective communication skills to produce the bottom-line results that will make you a winner.

Summary

In order to thrive in the diverse business environment of tomorrow, managers must be culturally sensitive. Improving your cultural sensitivity begins with self-awareness. This chapter presented two tools that will facilitate self-assessment of cultural sensitivity and help you set realistic, concrete goals. Next, we considered ways to translate cultural attitudes and values into managerial behaviors. Instead of a universalist approach, which calls for treating everyone the same, or a particularist approach,

Figure 11.3 Sequence for Success

which calls for individual treatment, managers need to be flexible and to accommodate the cultural values and practices of the workforce.

Finally, we examined strategies for developing cultural sensitivity in others, which include formal training, zero-tolerance for disrespect, openly discussing differences, and promoting the benefits of diversity. Following the Sequence for Success will enable you to use your effective communication skills to produce the bottom-line results that will make both you and your organization successful.

Endnotes

i. Milton J. Bennett (1986). "A Developmental Approach to Training for Intercultural Sensitivity," *International Journal of Intercultural Relations* 10, pp. 179–96.

ii. Michael Morris, Kwok Leung (2000). "Justice for All? Progress in Research on Cultural Variation in the Psychology of Distributive and Procedural Justice," *Applied Psychology: An International Review* 49, no. 1, pp. 100–32.

iii. Wallace V. Schmidt, Roger N. Conaway, Susan S. Easton, William J. Wardrope (2007). *Communicating Globally: Intercultural Communication and International Business* (Thousand Oaks, CA: Sage Publications), pp. 262–63.

iv. Bolchover, D. (2012). "Competing Across Borders: How Cultural and Communication Barriers Affect Business" (The Economist Intelligence Unit Ltd. Report).

v. Towers Watson (2013). "Change and Communication ROI Study Report: How the Fundamentals Have Evolved and the Best Adapt," Retrieved from www.towerswatson.com

vi. Project Management Institute, Inc. (2013, May). "PMI's Pulse of the Profession In-Depth: The Essential Role of Communication," Retrieved from www.pmi.org

APPENDIX 1

Managerial Communication Competencies Survey

©2015—Dr. Geraldine Hynes

Instructions: Rate yourself on each of the managerial communication competencies below by checking the appropriate box. When deciding on a rating, consider any feedback from your bosses, subordinates, and/or coworkers as well as your self-assessment.

	Weak	Fair	Average	Good	Excellent
Interpersonal Relations					
I convey warmth and empathy when communicating at work.					
I remain open-minded in work relationships.					
I resist judging or comparing people.					
I am sensitive to cultural differences.					
I foster liking and trust among my coworkers.					
Listening					
I am motivated to listen to others.					
I encourage people to give me feedback.					
I listen empathically and convey interest.					

(Continued)

	Weak	Fair	Average	Good	Excellent
I am alert to verbal and nonverbal cues.					
I use feedback techniques such as paraphrasing.					
Speaking					
I state my point simply and succinctly.					
I support my opinion with facts, reasons, or examples.					
I tailor my words to the level and experience of the listeners.					
I give clear, logically organized instructions.					
I know how to begin and conclude a business presentation.					
I organize my points logically and use transitions so listeners can follow me from point to point.					
My nonverbal behaviors are consistent with the verbal message.					
I use visual aids (e.g., PowerPoint) smoothly and appropriately.					
Asking Questions					
I know how to ask various types of questions for different purposes.					
I recognize hostility and resistance in question form.					
I check my understanding of a question before replying.					

	Weak	Fair	Average	Good	Excellent
Team Communication					
I interact cooperatively with teammates to achieve our goal.					
I can diagnose the problem when my team isn't working well.					
I understand the fundamentals of group dynamics.					
I can motivate and lead a team to achieve high performance.					

	Weak	Fair	Average	Good	Excellent
Interviews and Meetings					
I participate in job selection interviews satisfactorily (either as an interviewer or applicant).					
I participate in performance appraisal interviews satisfactorily (either as a supervisor or subordinate).					
I know how to begin and conclude an interview.					
I make valuable contributions to business meetings.					
I am competent in leading meetings.					
Writing Routine Business Documents					
I compose letters and memos in standard business format.					
I compose documents that are logically organized.					
I plan documents by considering my purpose and intended readers.					
I revise documents for conciseness, clarity, and completeness.					
My written messages have a courteous and professional tone.					
I use Standard American English grammar.					
I proofread documents for surface errors (spelling, mechanics).					
Writing Reports and Proposals					
I know how to compose all the parts of standard business reports and proposals.					
I can write an Executive Summary.					
I organize formal reports logically.					
I write persuasive proposals that achieve their goal.					
I use graphs and tables to clarify complex or technical information.					

	Weak	Fair	Average	Good	Excellent
Supervisor–Subordinate Communication					
I communicate goals in support of the company's mission.					
I enhance my subordinates' commitment to their work.					
I convey confidence in my subordinates' ability to be successful.					
I delegate responsibility and express trust.					
I allow my subordinates freedom to decide how they will accomplish the goals.					
I demonstrate support for organizational change.					
I gain my subordinates' support for ideas, projects, and solutions.					
I track progress against the goals and address performance problems promptly.					
I coach my subordinates to develop their capabilities.					
I pass on information to subordinates as appropriate.					
I notice, interpret, and anticipate my subordinates' concerns.					
I demonstrate concern for satisfying the company's internal and external customers.					
I make decisions in a timely manner and convey them to my subordinates.					

APPENDIX 2

Presentation Rubric

©2015—Dr. Geraldine Hynes

Content

Actual Pts	Possible Pts	Criteria	Comments
	10	Information is new and interesting.	
	20	Ideas are well-developed and supported with variety of material.	

Audience Adaptation

Actual Pts	Possible Pts	Criteria	Comments
	10	Info is tied to audience's interests and needs.	

Organization

Actual Pts	Possible Pts	Criteria	Comments
	5	Intro: attention-getter, purpose, credibility, motivation to listen, preview of points.	
	5	Body: 2–4 main points with support.	
	5	Conclusion: summary, importance, final thought.	
	5	Transitions connecting the parts.	

Visual Aids

Actual Pts	Possible Pts	Criteria	Comments
	10	Slides are well designed (colors, fonts, clipart) with no surface errors.	
	5	Slides contain helpful info, simply worded.	

Delivery

Actual Pts	Possible Pts	Criteria	Comments
	5	Speaker uses notes, not a script, and does not read the screen to the audience.	
	5	Speaker looks at audience, uses facial expressions, gestures, movement, and is appropriately dressed.	
	5	Voice is modulated for emphasis and variety.	
	5	Time is well used and within appropriate range.	

Question & Answer Session

Actual Pts	Possible Pts	Criteria	Comments
	5	Responsive, articulate answers are given.	

Total Score _____/100

Listener Feedback About Presentation

©2015—Dr. Geraldine Hynes

	Poor				Excellent
Content:					
Interest and relevance to you	1	2	3	4	5
Your understanding of the information provided	1	2	3	4	5
Freshness of the information	1	2	3	4	5
Organization: How well did the speaker...					
...begin with an attention-getter?	1	2	3	4	5
...state the purpose?	1	2	3	4	5
...have 2–4 clearly defined main points?	1	2	3	4	5
...support each main point?	1	2	3	4	5
...summarize and end with a look to the future?	1	2	3	4	5
Visual Aids: How effective was the visual aids'...					
...design (colors, fonts, readability, clip art)?	1	2	3	4	5
...content?	1	2	3	4	5
...handling?	1	2	3	4	5
Delivery: How effective was the presenter's...					
...voice?	1	2	3	4	5
...body language (gestures, movement)?	1	2	3	4	5
...eye contact?	1	2	3	4	5
...appearance (clothing, posture)?	1	2	3	4	5

Reviewer (optional): _____ Score: _____ / 75

APPENDIX 3

Work Plan Template

©2015—Dr. Geraldine Hynes

Purpose: To create a "script" for your improvement effort and support implementation.

Directions:

1. Using this form as a template, develop a work plan for each goal identified through the needs assessment process. Modify the form as needed to fit your unique context.
2. Distribute copies of each work plan to the members of the collaboration.
3. Keep copies handy to bring to meetings to review and update regularly. You may decide to develop new work plans for new phases of your reform effort.

Goal:

Results/Accomplishments:

Action Steps What will be done?	Responsibilities Who will do it?	Timeline By when? (Day/Month)	Resources A. Resources available B. Resources Needed (financial, human, political & other)	Potential Barriers A. What individuals or organizations might resist? B. How?	Communication Plan Who is involved? What methods? How often?
Step 1:			A. B.	A. B.	
Step 2:			A. B.	A. B.	
Step 3:			A. B.	A. B.	
Step 4:			A. B.	A. B.	
Step 5:			A. B.	A. B.	

Evidence Of Success (How will you know that you are making progress? What are your benchmarks?)

Evaluation Process (How will you determine that your goal has been reached? What are your measures?)

Bibliography

American Management Association (2014, June 2). "The Latest on Employee Surveillance," Retrieved from http://www.amanet.org/training/articles/ The-Latest-on-Workplace-Monitoring-and-Surveillance.aspx

Becker, B.E., Klimoski, R.J. (1989). "A Field Study of the Relationship Between the Organizational Feedback Environment and Performance," *Personnel Psychology* 42, no. 3, pp. 343–58.

Bennett, M.J. (1986). "A Developmental Approach to Training for Intercultural Sensitivity," *International Journal of Intercultural Relations* 10, pp. 179–96.

Bolchover, D. (2012). "Competing Across Borders: How Cultural and Communication Barriers Affect Business" (The Economist Intelligence Unit Ltd. Report).

Bradberry, T., Greaves, J. (2009). *Emotional Intelligence 2.0* (San Diego, CA: Talent Smart).

Bryant, A. (2014, August 3). "See Yourself as Others See You: Interview with Sharon Sloane," *New York Times*, p. 2.

Carroll, A.B. (2006, July 29). "Trust is the Key When Rating Great Workplaces," Retrieved from http://onlineathens.com/stories/073006/ business_20060730047.shtml, p. 1.

Cederblom, D. (1992). "The Performance Appraisal Interview: A Review, Implications, and Suggestions," in *Readings in Organizational Communication,* ed. K.L. Hutchinson (Dubuque, IA: Wm. C. Brown), pp. 310–21.

Colvin, G. (1999, July 19). "Outperforming the S&P 500: Companies that Pursue Diversity Outperform the S&P 500. Coincidence?" *Fortune* 140, no. 2.

Culbert, S.A. (2010). *Get Rid of the Performance Review! How Companies Can Stop Intimidating, Start Managing, and Focus on What Really Matters* (New York, NY: Hachette Book Group).

Donohue, W.A., Diez, M.E., Stahl, R.B. (1983). "New Directions in Negotiations Research," in *Communication Yearbook* 7, ed. R.N. Bostrom (Beverly Hills, CA: Sage Publications), pp. 249–79.

Downs, T.M. (1990). "Predictions of Communication Satisfaction during Performance Appraisal Interviews," *Management Communication Quarterly* 3, no. 13, pp. 334–54.

Dugan, B. (1988). "Effects of Assessor Training on Information Use," *Journal of Applied Psychology* 73, pp. 743–48.

Edelman (2012). "Edelman Trust Barometer: Executive Summary," Retrieved from http://www.scribd.com/doc/79026497/2012-Edelman-Trust-Barometer-Executive-Summary

Ekman, P., Friesen, W., Scherer, K.R. (1976). "Body Movement and Voice Pitch in Deception Interaction," *Semiotica* 16, no. 11, p. 26.

Elmuti, D., Davis, H.H. (2006). Not worth the bad will. *Industrial Management* 48, no. 6, pp. 26–30.

Erbert, L.A. (2014). "Antagonistic and Non-Antagonistic Dialectical Contradictions in Organizational Conflict," *International Journal of Business Communication* 51, no. 2, pp. 138–58.

Gammage, J. (2006, January 29). "Good Liars May be Wired Differently," *Houston Chronicle,* p. 2D.

Gibb, J.R. (1961). "Defensive Communication," *Journal of Communication,* September, pp. 141–48.

Gladwell, M. (2008). *Outliers: The Story of Success* (New York, NY: Little, Brown and Company), p. 175.

Goleman, D. (1995). *Emotional Intelligence* (New York, NY: Bantam Publishing Co.).

Gosling, S. (2008). *Snoop: What Your Stuff Says about You* (Profile Books), p. 13.

Grant, A. (2013). *Give and Take: A Revolutionary Approach to Success* (New York, NY: Viking Press), pp. 58–9.

Gudykunst, W.B. (1998). *Bridging Differences: Effective Intergroup Communication*, 3rd ed. (Thousand Oaks, CA: Sage Publications).

Hammill, G. (2005). "Mixing and Managing Four Generations of Employees," *FDR Magazine Online*, Retrieved from http://www.fdu.edu/newspubs/magazine/05ws/generations.htm

Hargie, O., Tourish, D., Wilson, N. (2001). "Communication Audits and the Effects of Increased Information: A Follow-Up Study," *Journal of Business Communication* 39, no. 4, pp. 414–36.

Hart Research Associates (2013). *It Takes More than a Major: Employer Priorities for College Learning and Student Success* (Washington, DC: Association of American Colleges and Universities).

Hoffman, L.R., Harburg, E., Meier, N.R.F. (1962). "Differences and Disagreements as Factors in Creative Problem-Solving," *Journal of Abnormal and Social Psychology* 64, no. 2, pp. 206–24.

Hofstede, G. (1980). "Motivation, Leadership and Organization: Do American Theories Apply Abroad?" *Organizational Dynamics* Summer, pp. 42–63.

Hsieh, T. (2013). *Delivering Happiness: A Path to Profits, Passion, and Purpose* (Grand Central Publishing).

Hughes, L. (2004, January–February). "Do's and Don'ts of Effective Team Leadership," *WIB, Magazine of the American Business Women's Association,* p. 10.

Hurst, A. (2014, April 20). "Being 'Good' Isn't the Only Way to Go," *Houston Chronicle,* p. B2.

Institute for the Future (2011). "Future Work Skills 2020" (Institute for the Future for the University of Phoenix Research Institute), Retrieved from www.iftf.org

Jayne, M.E.A., Dipboye, R. (2004, Winter). "Leveraging Diversity to Improve Business Performance: Research Findings and Recommendations for Organizations," *Human Resource Management* 43, no. 4, pp. 409–24.

Kameda, N. (2014). "Japanese Business Discourse of Oneness: A Personal Perspective," *International Journal of Business Communication* 51, no. 1, pp. 93–113.

Kirkpatrick, A. (2009). *World Englishes: Implications for International Communication and English Language Teaching* (Cambridge, England: Cambridge University Press).

Kochan, T., Bezrukova, K., Ely, R., Jackson, S., Joshi, A., Jehn, K., et al. (2003). "The Effects of Diversity on Business Performance: Report of the Diversity Research Network," *Human Resource Management* 42, pp. 3–21.

Krawcheck, S. (2014, March 24). "Diversify Corporate America," *Time*, pp. 36–7.

"Labor Force, Employment, and Earnings" (2012) (U.S. Census Bureau), Statistical Abstract of the United States, Table 616, p. 393.

"Leadership in Diversity and Inclusion" (2014, November 9), *New York Times Magazine*, pp. 54–8.

Lewis, P.V. (1987). *Organizational Communication: The Essence of Effective Management,* 3rd ed. (New York, NY: Wiley & Sons), pp. 46–48.

Lisa Guerin, J.D. (n.d.). "Monitoring Employee Communications: Learn the Rules on Monitoring Email, Voicemail, Telephone Conversations, and Internet Use," Retrieved from http://www.nolo.com/legal-encyclopedia/monitoring-employee-communications-29853.html

Lohr, S. (2014, June 21). "Unblinking Eyes Track Employees: Workplace Surveillance Sees Good and Bad," *New York Times,* Retrieved from http://www.nytimes.com/2014/06/22/technology/workplace-surveillance-sees-good-and-bad.html?_r=0

Maier, R.F. (1958). *The Appraisal Interview: Objectives and Skills* (New York, NY: John Wiley & Sons), p. 3.

McClintock, C.J., Hunt, R.G. (1975). "Nonverbal Indicators of Affect and Deception in Interview Situations," *Journal of Applied Psychology* 5, no. 3, p. 420.

McGregor, D. (1960). *The Human Side of Enterprise* (New York, NY: McGraw-Hill).

McWorthy, L., Henningsen, D.D. (2014). "Looking at Favorable and Unfavorable Superior-Subordinate Relationships through Dominance and

Affiliation Lenses," *International Journal of Business Communication* 51, no. 2, pp. 123–37.

Mishra, K., Boynton, L., Mishra, A. (2014). "Driving Employee Engagement: the Expanded Role of Internal Communications," *International Journal of Business Communication* 51, no. 2, pp. 183–202.

Morris, M., Leung, K. (2000). "Justice for All? Progress in Research on Cultural Variation in the Psychology of Distributive and Procedural Justice," *Applied Psychology: An International Review* 49, no. 1, pp. 100–32.

Munter, M. (2012). *Guide to Managerial Communication: Effective Business Writing and Speaking*, 9th ed. (Upper Saddle River, NJ: Prentice Hall), p. 154.

Neuliep, J.W. (2012). *Intercultural Communication: A contextual Approach*, 5th ed. (Thousand Oaks, CA: Sage Publications), pp. 374–5.

Nisbett, R. (2004). *The Geography of Thought: How Asians and Westerners Think Differently…and Why* (Free Press).

Project Management Institute, Inc. (2013). "The High Cost of Low Performance: The Essential Role of Communications" (Pulse of the Profession In-depth Report), Retrieved from www.pmi.org

Putnam, L., Wilson, S. (1988). "Argumentation and Bargaining Strategies as Discriminators of Integrative and Distributive Outcomes," in *Managing Conflict: An Interdisciplinary Approach,* ed. A. Rahim (New York, NY: Praeger Publishers).

Quirk, B. (2008). *Making the Connections: Using Internal Communication To Turn Strategy Into Action* (Burlington, VT: Gower), p. 102.

Radicati Group (2014). "Email Statistics Report, 2013–2017," Retrieved from http://www.radicati.com/wp/wp_content/uploads/2013/04/Email-Statistics-Report-2013-2017-Executive -Summary.pdf

Ramirez-Esparza, N., Gosling, S.D., Benet-Martinez, V., Potter, J.P., Pennebaker, J.W. (2006). "Do Bilinguals have Two Personalities? A Special Case of Cultural Frame Switching," *Journal of Research in Personality* 40, pp. 99–120.

Rasberry, R. (2013, March 15). "A Study of How Fortune 100 Companies Communicate Ethics, Governance, Corporate Responsibility, Sustainability, and Human Rights," Paper Presented at the Association for Business Communication-Southwestern U.S. Annual Conference, Albuquerque, NM.

Robison, J. (2012, January 5). "Boosting Engagement at Stryker," *Gallup Management Journal,* Retrieved from http://gmj.gallup.com/content/150956/Boosting-Engagement-Stryker.aspx, p. 1.

Ross, H.J. (2014, August 3). "An Appeal to Our Inner Judge," *New York Times*, p. D3.

Rothfelder, J. (2014). *Driving Honda: Inside the World's Most Innovative Car Company* (New York: Portfolio/Penguin), p. 134.

Russ, G.S., Daft, R.L., Lengel, R.H. (1990). "Media Selection and Managerial Characteristics in Organizational Communications," *Management Communication Quarterly* 4, no. 2, pp. 151–75.

Sarnoff, N. (2014, June 13). "Younger Workers Crave 'Sense of Place' on the Job," *Houston Chronicle*, p. D1.

Schmidt, W.V., Conaway, R.N., Easton, S.S., Wardrope, W.J. (2007). *Communicating Globally: Intercultural Communication and International Business* (Thousand Oaks, CA: Sage Publications), pp. 262–63.

Schroeder, J., Risen, J.L. (2014, July 28). "Befriending the Enemy: Outgroup Friendship Longitudinally Predicts Intergroup Attitudes in a Coexistence Program for Israelis and Palestinians," *Group Processes and Intergroup Relations Journal*, doi: 10.1177/1368430214542257.

Schwartz, T., Porath, C. (2014, June 1). "Why You Hate Work," *New York Times*, p. 1SR.

Shafiq, M., Zia-ur-Rehman, M., Rashid, M. (2013). "Impact of Compensation, Training and Development and Supervisory Support on Organizational Commitment," *Compensation and Benefits Review* 45, no. 5, pp. 278–85.

Sias, P.M., Krone, K.J., Jablin, F.M. (2002). "An Ecological Systems Perspective on Workplace Relationships," in *Handbook of Interpersonal Communication*, 3rd ed., eds. M.L. Knapp, J.A. Daly (Thousand Oaks, CA: Sage Publications), pp. 615–42.

Sigband, N., Bell, A. (1986). *Communicating for Management and Business*, 4th ed. (Glenview, IL: Scott Foresman), pp. 69–70.

Sigmar, L.S., Hynes, G.E., Hill, K.L. (2012). "Strategies for Teaching Social and Emotional Intelligence in Business Communication," *Business Communication Quarterly* 75, no. 3, pp. 301–17.

"Silicon Valley's Diversity Problem" (2014, October 5). *New York Times*, p. SR10.

Sixel, I.M. (2013, May 16). "Permission to Speak Freely to the Boss," *Houston Chronicle*, 2013, p. D1.

Sotomayor, S. (2014). *My Beloved World* (New York, NY: Vintage Books), pp. 199, 123.

Tannen, D. (2007). *You Just Don't Understand: Women and Men in Conversation* (New York, NY: William Morrow).

The Present (and Future) of Business Communications" (2005, July 25). *Accounting Web*, Retrieved from http://www.accountingweb.com

Thomas, G.F., Zolin, R., Hartman, J.L. (2009). "The Central Role of Communication in Developing Trust and Its Effect on Employee Involvement," *Journal of Business Communication* 46, no. 3, pp. 287–310.

Toossi, M. (2013, December). "Labor Force Projections to 2022," *Monthly Labor Review*, Retrieved from www.bls.gov/EMP

Towers Watson (2013). "Change and Communication ROI Study Report: How the Fundamentals Have Evolved and the Best Adapt," Retrieved from www.towerswatson.com.

Vickery, H.B. (1984, January). "Tapping into the Employee Grapevine," *Association Management,* pp. 59–64.

Waltman, J.L. (1983). "Nonverbal Interrogation: Some Applications," *Journal of Police Science and Administration* 11, no. 2, p. 167.

Wen, H.J., Schwieger, D., Gershuny, P. (2007). "Internet Usage Monitoring In the Workplace: Its Legal Challenges and Implementation Strategies," *Information Systems Management* 24, no. 2, pp. 185–96.

Wood, J.T. (2013). *Gendered Lives: Communication, Gender, and Culture,* 10th ed. (Boston: Wadsworth), p. 127.

Index

OTHER TITLES IN OUR CORPORATE COMMUNICATION COLLECTION

Debbie DuFrene, Editor

- *Managing Investor Relations: Strategies for Effective Communication* By Alexander Laskin
- *Fundamentals of Writing for Marketing and Public Relations: A Step-by-Step Guide for Quick and Effective Results* By Janet Mizrahi
- *Managing Virtual Teams* By Debbie DuFrene and Carol Lehman
- *Corporate Communication: Tactical Guidelines for Strategic Practice* By Michael Goodman and Peter B. Hirsch
- *Communication Strategies for Today's Managerial Leader* By Deborah Roebuck
- *Communication in Responsible Business: Strategies, Concepts, and Cases* By Roger N. Conaway and Oliver Laasch
- *Managerial Communication: Evaluating the Right Dose* By J. David Johnson
- *Web Content: A Writer's Guide* By Janet Mizrahi
- *Intercultural Communication for Managers* By Michael B. Goodman
- *Persuasive Business Presentations: Using the Problem-Solution Method to Influence Decision Makers to Take Action* By Gary May
- *SPeak Performance: Using the Power of Metaphors to Communicate Vision, Motivate People, and Lead Your Organization to Success* By Jim Walz
- *Today's Business Communication: A How-To Guide for the Modern Professional* By Jason L. Snyder and Robert Forbus
- *Leadership Talk: A Discourse Approach to Leader Emergence* By Robyn Walker and Jolanta Aritz
- *Communication Beyond Boundaries* By Payal Mehra
- *Managerial Communication* By Reginald L. Bell and Jeanette S. Martin

Announcing the Business Expert Press Digital Library

Concise e-books business students need for classroom and research

This book can also be purchased in an e-book collection by your library as

- *a one-time purchase,*
- *that is owned forever,*
- *allows for simultaneous readers,*
- *has no restrictions on printing, and*
- *can be downloaded as PDFs from within the library community.*

Our digital library collections are a great solution to beat the rising cost of textbooks. E-books can be loaded into their course management systems or onto students' e-book readers. The **Business Expert Press** digital libraries are very affordable, with no obligation to buy in future years. For more information, please visit **www.businessexpertpress.com/librarians**. To set up a trial in the United States, please contact **sales@businessexpertpress.com**